THE
QUICK AFTER-WORK
SUMMER
VEGETARIAN
COOKBOOK

THE
QUICK AFTER-WORK
SUMMER
VEGETARIAN
COOKBOOK

Hilaire Walden

PIATKUS

First published in 1996 by
Judy Piatkus (Publishers) Ltd
5 Windmill Street, London W1P 1HF

The moral right of the author has been asserted
*A catalogue record for this book is available from
the British Library*

ISBN 0–7499–1590–0

Designed by Paul Saunders
Illustrations by Madeleine David

Cover photograph by Steve Baxter shows
Greek Beach Grill (page 32),
Green, Red, Black and White Pilaff (page 104) and
Figs with Raspberry Sauce (page 121)

Data capture by Create Publishing Services, Bath
Printed and bound in Great Britain by
Bookcraft Ltd, Midsomer Norton, Avon

CONTENTS

Introduction

In summer most people want to spend as little time as possible indoors cooking, preferring to be in the sun and open air, whether simply lazing in the garden or taking part in some more energetic activity. If you go out to work rather than working from home, you will probably have an even greater lack of incentive to cook; very few premises are air-conditioned, and the journey home can be the last straw.

Please resist the temptation to buy ready prepared food. There really is no need. As the recipes on the following pages show you do not have to spend hours over a hot stove to prepare appetising home-made dishes. They can be ready in the time it takes to heat or cook bought ones. What's more, food you have prepared and cooked yourself has a number of plusses. It can be cheaper, your hands and utensils are the only ones that have touched your food, you know what has gone into each dish, and it is eaten, or cooked and eaten, immediately it is prepared unlike ready prepared food that will have sat around and then travelled in your shopping basket in the same (possibly high) temperatures as yourself.

Many of the recipes I have chosen for this book come from the Mediterranean. This is because Mediterranean food is natural for summer eating. It bursts with so much sun, colour, flavour and wonderful aromas that it is impossible to resist. The emphasis is on taste, and as the best Mediterranean food emanates from the kitchens of ordinary people, it is unpretentious and simple. With no complicated, fancy techniques or involved methods, it is ideal for the cook in a hurry.

The Mediterranean diet has recently been acclaimed for its healthiness, and vegetarians have always been well catered for in the region's cooking. This is because meat has always been scarce, and its consumption has further been limited by religious laws that proscribe it on fast days and often limit choice. However, the wonderful array of vegetables plus a wealth of grains and pulses – all of which are used in simple ways, with panache, to produce dishes that belie their simplicity – mean that meat is not missed. Barbecuing is an increasingly popular way of cooking and vegetables cooked by this method can be served in innumerable ways, as snacks, first courses, main courses and accompaniments. In this book you will find plenty of recipes that you can cook on a barbecue when your time is not at a premium.

I have cooked all the recipes, except sometimes the risottos, happily and at my leisure, in less than 30 minutes. Most take much less time. A risotto can be ready in 20–25 minutes, but could take up to 35 minutes of almost undivided attention. To save frustration and valuable time, I check that I have everything I need before starting a recipe, remove from the refrigerator any ingredients that are to be used, if I have not already done so, (fridge-cold ingredients take longer to cook), and check the recipe method.

For the most efficient use of your time in the kitchen, and to allow you more time to spend outside or enjoying some other activity – or inactivity – I have worked out which ingredients can be prepared while others are cooking. Because I have included all these individual chopping, slicing, etc. instructions in the methods, they can sometimes appear deceptively time-consuming. In fact, if the recipe was written and made in the conventional way, with all the preparation done before cooking commenced, it would take longer.

If you are planning to serve two or more courses, check that they don't require constant attention at the same time. Instead, choose recipes that can be dove-tailed together. See the menu suggestions on pages 129–134 for ideas.

I do hope that the following collection of recipes will prove that you can quickly, easily and coolly prepare your own interesting food that is just right for summer eating and life styles. I also hope that you will adopt the experimental approach to my recipes and make your own modifications if you prefer a slightly different method or taste, or do not have one of the ingredients.

Recipes suitable for vegans carry the following symbol Ⓥ.

Equipment

Everything that is needed for the recipes in this book will be found in all but the most basic kitchens. You don't even need an oven as very few of the dishes are baked. Below are a few notes that I hope you will find helpful.

KNIVES

One reasonably sharp knife is all that is really necessary to prepare the recipes in this book adequately, although a larger range could help you to work more efficiently – provided the knives are sharp. Using a blunt knife is a waste of time. Knives now retain their sharpness for longer than those of yesteryear and modern knife-sharpeners are easier to use than traditional steel ones; some knives come in their own blade-sharpening scabbard.

BLENDER

A small blender is more versatile than a large one because it is useful for grinding spices and making many of the sauces in this book, which a large one cannot do. It is also a suitable size when catering for two people, which applies to much quick cooking. While a larger one is better for soups and dips, it is not too time-consuming to purée these in batches in the smaller one. A small blender also takes up less space so is easier to store; it is also easier to wash and dry.

FRYING PANS

For ease and for the best results and the efficient use of heat, it is a good idea to use a small frying pan for cooking small amounts, and a large, deep-sided one for large amounts such as Ratatouille (see page 35) and for frittate and tortillas. Both pans should have heavy bases. A non-stick coating reduces the amount of oil that is needed and makes cooking and washing up easier, but it can be damaged by sharp implements and by being used over a high heat, particularly if the pan is dry.

MANDOLIN

A metal, wooden or plastic mandolin with an adjustable steel blade makes quick, neat work of slicing and grating vegetables. It takes up less room and is easier to wash up than a food processor and is less prone to reducing foods such as onions to a mush. It is also cheaper.

MEZZALUNA

A mezzaluna is very useful for chopping herbs, garlic, onions, nuts, etc. if you are not very proficient with a knife. It is a sickle-shaped blade with a handle at each end. Mezzalunas are available in a range of sizes.

PESTLE AND MORTAR

Unless I am doing a large batch of spices, I use a pestle and mortar for crushing them – it only takes a moment. Alternatively, you can use the end of a rolling pin and a bowl.

POTATO PEELER

As well as peeling vegetables, a potato peeler comes in handy for shaving off thin slithers of Parmesan cheese.

SAUCEPANS

A large saucepan is needed to cook pasta and rice. Heavy-based or non-stick pans are required for 'stewy' dishes such as Broad Beans and Potatoes Braised in Tomatoes (see page 92) that would traditionally have been cooked slowly for a long time.

Ingredients

All the ingredients I have used should be readily available in medium and large branches of all good supermarkets and many independent shops. If you cannot find something you want on the shelves, ask the shop or department manager or supervisor for it.

BULGAR

Also called 'burghul' in the Middle East and 'pourgouri' in Turkey, nutty tasting bulgar is made from hulled wheat grains that are cracked by boiling and then dried. (True cracked wheat is not the same – it is simply the cracked grain, requires cooking and does not have such a nutty flavour.) Bulgar is ideal for the cook in a hurry as it only needs to be rehydrated and perhaps warmed. Rehydration can be done by soaking in cold water for 15 minutes if the bulgar is to be served cold, or by simmering or soaking in hot water for 2–5 minutes respectively if it is to be served hot. It must then be squeezed hard to expel excess moisture.

Bulgar is a quick, interesting and foolproof alternative to rice and can be flavoured and used in the same ways as pilaff-style dishes (see pages 101–104). If you have the choice, use fine grain bulgar for salads such as Tabbouleh (see page 82) and coarse grain bulgar for pilaffs.

COUSCOUS

Couscous is made from semolina that has been ground, moistened and rolled in flour. It used to require quite lengthy and laborious preparation and heating but the vast majority of couscous that is now sold in ethnic shops and in supermarkets is pre-cooked and needs only to be moistened, heated through and the grains separated. Butter or oil is usually rubbed into the grains to help to do this and to enrich them.

EGGS

Throughout most of my life I have eaten eggs from hens that have roamed free in a farmyard, in a paddock and occasionally in a garden. They actually have a flavour, which is more than can be said for nearly all, if not all, battery eggs. I like the yolks of my boiled and poached eggs to be runny and my scrambled eggs, omelettes and frittata to be creamy – just what 'experts' tell me I shouldn't eat for risk of getting salmonella food poisoning. Yet I have never suffered even the slightest sign of sickness or stomach ache after eating eggs cooked like this. I always do know their source and always collect or buy them soon after they have been laid. However, the young, pregnant, elderly and those suffering, or recovering from, major illness are more susceptible to salmonella so it may be as well if they do not eat lightly cooked eggs.

HARISSA

Harissa is a fiery Tunisian paste that is used quite liberally in that country's cooking and is often put on the table as a condiment. Recipes vary and some have a more noticeable spiciness, as well as heat, than others. Harissa also now appears in other North African countries and in the Middle East. It can be bought in traditional paste form as well as in a powder, from specialist food shops and some supermarkets, but it can be made very quickly and easily at home.

25g/1oz dried red chillies
1 clove garlic, crushed
1 teaspoon coriander seeds
1 teaspoon cumin seeds
1 teaspoon caraway seeds
a pinch of salt
2½–3 tablespoons olive oil

Soak the chillies in hot water in a covered bowl for 1 hour. Drain them and put into a mortar, spice grinder or small blender with the garlic, coriander, cumin and caraway seeds and salt. Mix to a paste, then stir in 2 table-spoons of the oil. Transfer to a small bowl or jar and pour the remaining oil over the surface. Keep in a cool, dry place for one day before using.

If stored in a cool, dark dry place, harissa will last for up to four months.

HERBS

I always use fresh herbs because their flavour is so much better than that of dried ones. Many are easy to grow in the garden, in tubs, or in pots kept on a sunny windowsill. They are also readily available, either cut or growing, in supermarkets and greengrocers. The flavour and pungency of any fresh herb can vary according to its growing conditions and the time of year, so it is a good idea to get into the habit of sampling a leaf from each different batch to assess how much you will need to use.

Store freshly cut herbs in 'stay fresh' bags that can be bought from healthfood shops and some supermarkets. If you are lucky enough to have more herbs than you can use, freeze them in small batches in labelled plastic bags.

The parsley used throughout this book is the flat-leaved kind.

OLIVE OIL

Colour is a good guide to strength of flavour, although it is not necessarily an indication of quality.

The range and diversity of olive oils is enormous – some can be richly fruity while others are surprisingly peppery. For a start, they are available in a range of qualities – simple 'olive oil', virgin olive oil and extra virgin olive oil. Then there are different oils from individual producers which, like good wine, vary from producer to producer and from year to year.

It is best to buy small bottles of different varieties and choose the ones you like. You can be extravagant and have a selection that allows you to match grades and flavours to specific dishes, but I suggest that a light, ordinary olive oil for cooking, a virgin olive oil for most salads and extra virgin olive oil for special salads and trickling on good bread is a good basis.

Keep olive oil in a cool, dark place to preserve its flavour.

PEPPERS

Like anything that has been grown, peppers vary. Freshness, fullness of flavour and fleshiness are the most important qualities. The first two can be judged by smell, the third by weight and, with experience, appearance: a pepper should feel heavy for its size and the flesh should not look thin (it is surprisingly easy to tell).

PULSES

This is the collective name for dried peas, beans and lentils. Fortuitously for the vegetarian cook in a hurry, pulses are one of the few ingredients that survive the canning process successfully, and I always have cans of kidney beans, chick peas and Italian cannellini and borlotti beans in my cupboard for making dips, salads and main courses. When I have no idea of what I am going to cook, I often use the pulse as the starting point, then simply add other ingredients and flavourings that I happen to have. In this way, I have created some extremely successful recipes.

Drain and rinse canned pulses to remove all the canning liquid.

Green lentils, especially those from Le Puy, do not require soaking and take only 15–20 minutes to cook, depending on the variety, how they have been dried and how fresh they are.

SPICES

You will not need a wide range of spices for the recipes in this book. Cumin and cardamom are the main ones I have used plus, on one or two occasions each, paprika pepper, coriander seeds, cayenne pepper (Tabasco sauce could be substituted), cinnamon and allspice.

For preference, buy whole spices as they are fresher tasting and last longer than ready ground ones. If ground spices are called for in a recipe, it takes only a couple of minutes to toast whole spices in a dry frying pan until they are fragrant, then tip them into a small blender and grind them. Keep spices in airtight containers in a cool, dark place for no more than four to six months.

SUN-DRIED TOMATO PASTE

I use sun-dried tomato paste instead of tomato purée to boost the flavour of tomato dishes, if necessary, because the paste has a richer, more complex flavour. Ordinary tomato purée can spoil the fresh taste of quickly cooked tomatoes and completely dominate a dish; it is more acceptable for recipes that require slow simmering. A number of different brands of sun-dried tomato paste are available, so shop around to find the one that you like.

SUN-DRIED TOMATOES

Only buy sun-dried tomatoes that have been dried naturally in the hot Mediterranean sun. Avoid ones that seem a bargain – if they are cheap they are not worth the money.

I have used sun-dried tomatoes that have been steeped in oil for my recipes. It is cheaper to buy dry tomatoes than ones packed commercially in oil, so soak a batch of dry ones in hot water for 1–1½ hours, drain them and then dry them with paper towels, then layer them in a jar with olive oil. Seal the jar and keep in a cool, dark place. The oil from the tomatoes can be used for salad dressings, in cooking and trickled on to good bread.

TAHINI

Also spelt 'tahina', this is a paste made from ground, toasted sesame seeds. Brands differ in their flavour so it may be worth trying a few to find the one that most suits your taste. Tahini separates when left for a while; stirring it back together in the jar can be quite difficult so I usually leave the jar standing on its lid to make blending easier. As with other nut and seed products, to delay rancidity, keep tahini in a cool, dark place – preferably not the refrigerator because the tahini will be even more difficult to blend together if separated.

TOMATOES

I have such a passion for raw tomatoes that borders on an addiction and eat them neat even they are not very well flavoured. (I think the only ones I was not tempted to eat after the first one were hothouse-grown Dutch cherry tomatoes, even though I was standing in the hothouse surrounded by them and could have eaten as many as I wanted. However, when it comes to tomatoes, especially cooked ones, in recipes, I like them to smell and taste as if they have just been plucked from a vine that has basked in the sun. Supermarkets have realised that many other people also want this

8

and it is now not difficult to buy tomatoes that are well-flavoured. I like large, ridged ones for cooking because they are so fleshy.

I'm not very keen on the taste of canned tomatoes and as it is now possible to buy fresh tomatoes with flavour all year round, the old reason for using the canned version, especially in winter – tasteless tomatoes – is less likely to be valid. If the flavour of fresh tomatoes does need boosting, I prefer to use sun-dried tomatoes or sun-dried tomato paste. On the one or two occasions when the extra liquid of canned tomatoes is needed for a dish, I use good quality ones (canned tomatoes do vary quite a lot in quality), price is invariably an indication.

Plum tomatoes do not necessarily taste better than others; they only do so if they are a traditional variety that has been ripened in the sunny south. Growers in more northerly countries cottoned on to the good reputation of plum tomatoes, as they did to that of ridged tomatoes a few years ago, and have been growing inferior varieties in less sunny climates.

If cooked tomatoes, tomato relishes, sauces, etc. are lacking in flavour, I boost the taste with sun-dried tomato paste, or a pinch of sugar.

To peel and seed tomatoes, put them in a bowl, pour boiling water over them and leave for one minute. Drain them, then, when the tomatoes are cool enough to handle, slip off the skins. Cut the tomatoes in half and scoop out the seeds with a teaspoon.

YOGURT

For the best results, use Greek strained ewe's milk yogurt. It has a unique mild, creamy flavour with just a hint of acidity. It is now widely available so there is no excuse for not using it. Strained cow's milk yogurt fails by quite a long way to imitate it and ordinary cow's milk yogurt fails even more drastically.

CHAPTER 1

Soups, First Courses & Snacks

This chapter contains a wide range of dishes: soups, pastries, dips, grilled mixed vegetable dishes, things on toast and bread and egg dishes. Many of them are Mediterranean in origin and some of these are traditionally more likely to be served in groups, rather than singly. However, they do make good individual dishes for first courses or snacks. A selection can also be served as a complete meal. Soups can be served as light meals, partnered by good bread and with cheese to follow. It is a long chapter for these reasons, and also because what on one occasion I might eat as a snack, on another I might serve as a first course and yet another, I might have it as a light lunch or supper with suitable accompaniments.

When it is hot I do not feel like spending much time cooking, so it is fortunate that summer is the time when many people are happy to have a snack or a snack-type meal rather than a full lunch or dinner.

GAZPACHO ⓥ

SERVES 4

Gazpacho is one of the glories of the cooking of Andalusia. As might be expected of a dish from this sun-baked region, it is a wonderfully cooling soup, just right for beginning a meal on a hot day. A further incentive for making gazpacho is that it does not require any cooking.

Although it is now always served as a first course, it used to be served after the main course and before the fruit. The proportions of vegetables are merely a guide and can be changed according to your taste and the taste of the particular ingredients you are using. To intensify the flavour, you could use tomato juice instead of water, or add some sun-dried tomato paste. Chill the bowls and add ice cubes to the soup.

½ cucumber, peeled
675g (1½lb) ripe, really well-flavoured tomatoes, peeled, deseeded and coarsely chopped
1 large red or green pepper, coarsely chopped
1 red onion, chopped
1–2 cloves garlic, chopped
5 tablespoons virgin olive oil
2 tablespoons red wine vinegar
100g (3½oz) fresh breadcrumbs

300–425ml (10–15fl oz) iced water
salt and freshly ground black pepper
sun-dried tomato paste, sugar or red wine vinegar (optional)

To serve
some or all of the following:
diced red or green pepper
diced cucumber
diced red onion
diced tomatoes

1. Put the vegetables, garlic, oil, vinegar, breadcrumbs and a little of the water into a food processor and mix together to leave some texture.

2. Add enough water to make a thick soup consistency and season to taste.

3. Chill for as long as possible. Before serving, taste to see if the flavour is right and add sun-dried tomato paste, sugar, vinegar or more seasoning if necessary.

4. Serve with the garnishes in separate small bowls.

Cucumber, Mint and Yogurt Soup

Serves 4

This refreshing soup takes just a matter of minutes to prepare and requires no cooking so, providing you use well-chilled yogurt, your first course can be ready in five minutes. If you think about it, pop the soup bowls into the refrigerator so that they are also nice and cold.

1–2 cloves garlic	about 1½ tablespoons chopped mint
1 cucumber, coarsely chopped	squeeze of lemon juice
450ml/16fl oz chilled Greek yogurt	salt and freshly ground black pepper
finely grated zest of 1 small lemon	mint leaves for garnish

1. With the motor running, drop the garlic into a blender or food processor, followed by the cucumber and 100ml 3½fl oz cold water.

2. Tip into a bowl and stir in the yogurt, lemon zest and mint and add lemon juice and seasoning to taste.

3. If you are not going to eat the soup straightaway, chill it until required. Serve in cold bowls, garnished with the mint leaves.

PARSLEY SOUP

SERVES 4

This soup is a verdant green (providing it is not over-boiled after the parsley is added), which was appropriate to the time of year when I first ate it: spring.

2 tablespoons olive oil
2 fat leeks, white parts only, chopped
1 large potato
570ml (1 pint) vegetable stock

leaves from 2 large bunches of parsley
300ml (½ pint) milk
salt and freshly ground black pepper

1. Heat the oil in a saucepan, add the leeks and fry until soft.

2. Dice the potato and stir into the softened leeks. Leave to cook, uncovered, over a low heat, stirring occasionally, for 10 minutes.

3. Add the stock, bring to the boil and simmer, uncovered, for about 15 minutes until the potato is tender, adding the parsley 2 minutes before the end of cooking.

4. Add the milk to the soup and purée in a blender or food processor, or press through a sieve. Return to the pan, season to taste and reheat. Do not allow to boil.

GARLIC SOUP

SERVES 4

The fresher the garlic cloves, the better. If you are really pressed for time, the frying of the garlic can be omitted but the soup will have a less complex flavour. If you cook the croûtes under the grill, make sure they do not become brown too quickly. For an extra savoury note, top the baked croûtes with freshly grated cheese.

4 tablespoons virgin olive oil	2 egg yolks
15 cloves garlic	5 tablespoons crème fraîche
850ml (1½ pints) vegetable stock	salt and freshly ground black pepper
4 slices of baguette	plenty of chopped parsley to garnish

1. Preheat the oven to 180°C/350°F/Gas Mark 4, or preheat the grill. Heat the oil in a saucepan, add the garlic and cover and cook until it is lightly coloured and softened. Add the stock and simmer, uncovered, for 15 minutes.

2. Meanwhile, either put the bread on a baking sheet and bake for 7–10 minutes, or toast under the grill, until golden and crisp throughout. Put a slice in each of four warm soup bowls. Keep warm.

3. Purée the soup in a blender or food processor, or press through a sieve. Return to the pan. Beat the egg yolks with the crème fraîche. Stir in a little of the soup, then pour it into the pan.

4. Heat gently, stirring, until the soup begins to thicken; do not allow to boil.

5. Season and pour into the bowls. Garnish with the chopped parsley.

COURGETTE AND MINT SOUP Ⓥ

SERVES 4–6

Making soup should not be seen as a good way of using up large courgettes; neither the flavour nor the colour of the soup will be as good as if you used small, fresh ones. Also, from the short-of-time cook's point of view, small ones cook more quickly, which is a further bonus for the colour.

If you think ahead, this soup is also very good served chilled.

1 tablespoon olive oil
1 onion, chopped
1 clove garlic, crushed
1kg (2lb) small or medium courgettes,
   sliced

1.1 litres (2 pints) vegetable stock
1 tablespoon chopped mint
salt and freshly ground black pepper
mint leaves, and 2 tablespoons cream
   (optional) to garnish

1. Heat the oil in a saucepan, add the onion, garlic and courgettes and cook gently, stirring occasionally, until they are soft.

2. Add the stock, bring to the boil then simmer for about 10 minutes. Add the mint and seasoning.

3. Allow the soup to cool slightly then purée in a blender or food processor. Return to the pan and reheat gently (take care not to overheat as the colour will be spoilt).

4. Garnish the soup with the mint leaves and a swirl of cream, if liked.

SOUPS, FIRST COURSES & SNACKS

Aubergine Soup

Aubergine soup has an enticing, subtle and unusual flavour but it is not the most attractive of soups if served ungarnished. Instead of the parsley sauce given here, you could use Rouille (see page 25); both complement the flavour of the soup as well as adding a splash of colour. Either sauce is also good spread on the bread that is eaten with the soup. When you have time, grill or bake the aubergine until the flesh is soft and the skin charred and blistered. This will add an attractive, smoky flavour. Purée the aubergine, skin and all.

2 tablespoons virgin olive oil

1 onion, chopped

1 plump clove garlic

1 aubergine weighing about 450g (1lb)

850ml (1½ pints) vegetable stock

salt and freshly ground black pepper

Parsley Sauce

2 cloves garlic

leaves from a bunch of parsley

3 tablespoons virgin olive oil

3 tablespoons freshly grated Parmesan cheese

1–3 teaspoons lemon juice to taste

1. Heat the oil in a saucepan, add the onion and fry gently for about 15–20 minutes.

2. Meanwhile, chop the garlic and aubergine and stir into the onion as soon as they are prepared, while it is cooking.

3. Meanwhile, make the parsley sauce by dropping the garlic cloves into a blender while the motor is running, then adding the parsley leaves, followed by the oil. Add the Parmesan, mix very briefly, then add lemon juice and seasoning to taste.

4. Tip the vegetables into a blender or food processor and add a little of the stock. Mix to a purée then return to the pan and stir in the remaining stock. Reheat and season to taste.

5. Serve each portion of soup with some of the sauce spooned on top.

Butternut Squash Soup Ⓥ

SERVES 4

This is a sunny, bright orange soup with a delicate taste highlighted by a hint of cumin. Butternut squash, which have now become quite widely available in supermarkets and grocers, are a summer version of pumpkin with a far superior flavour. You may have to buy two squash to get the weight. If liked, you could swirl crème fraîche, Greek yogurt or cream through the soup just before serving, and garnish with coriander leaves. Garlic or cheese croûtons make a good accompaniment.

40g (1½oz) unsalted butter
1 onion, chopped
about 900g (2lb) butternut squash

¾ teaspoon cumin seeds
850ml (1½ pints) vegetable stock
salt and freshly ground black pepper

1. Heat the butter in a saucepan, add the onion and cook gently until softened.

2. Meanwhile, peel the squash, discard the seeds and chop the flesh fairly finely.

3. Stir the cumin seeds into the onion for about 1 minute then add the squash and stock. Bring to the boil, cover and simmer for about 15 minutes until the squash is tender.

4. Allow the soup to cool slightly then purée in a blender or food processor, or pass through a sieve.

5. Return the soup to the pan, reheat and season to taste.

BEAN, TOMATO AND CORIANDER SOUP Ⓥ

SERVES 3–4

Authentically, white kidney beans would be used for this Middle Eastern soup, but the flavour and texture of Italian cannellini beans seem to marry better with the other ingredients. The sauce really sets off the soup.

1 plump clove garlic, chopped
2 tablespoons virgin olive oil
1 bay leaf
1 onion
1 red pepper
4 large well-flavoured ripe tomatoes
2 × 425g (15oz) cans white kidney or
　cannellini beans

850ml (1½ pints) vegetable stock
salt and freshly ground black pepper

Sauce
3 plump cloves garlic
a large handful of mixed coriander and
　parsley leaves
75ml (3fl oz) extra virgin oil

1. Simmer the garlic for the sauce just covered by water in a small saucepan, for 10 minutes.

2. While this is happening, start to prepare the soup. Heat the oil in a saucepan, add the garlic and bay leaf and heat while you finely chop the onion. Add it to the pan and leave to cook until softened.

3. Meanwhile, finely chop the pepper and chop the tomatoes. Add to the softened onions and cook for 5 minutes.

4. Drain and rinse the beans, add to the pan with the stock, bring to the boil then simmer, uncovered, for about 10 minutes. Season to taste.

5. Drain the garlic for the sauce and drop into a small blender or food processor and mix with the coriander and parsley. With the motor running, slowly pour in the oil. Season to taste.

6. Serve each portion of soup with a spoonful of sauce.

AUBERGINE DIP ⓥ

SERVES 4

After eating this dish innumerable times I came across this version which I instantly decided I preferred to all the others – the aubergine is not reduced to a smooth purée but has a nubbly texture. Make it as far in advance of eating it as you can to allow the flavours to mature, but do not put it in the refrigerator (unless you are preparing it several hours ahead) as it should be served at room temperature.

---

2 small aubergines
2 cloves garlic
2 tablespoons extra virgin olive oil
2 tablespoons chopped parsley or
 coriander
1–2 tablespoons lemon juice
a pinch of ground cumin

about 25g (1oz) red onion, very finely
 chopped
salt and freshly ground black pepper
olive oil and chopped parsley or coriander
 to garnish
warm pitta bread to serve

---

1. Preheat the grill. Cut deep slashes in the aubergines and insert the garlic well into the flesh. Grill the aubergines, turning frequently for 15–20 minutes until the skins are blackened and blistered and the aubergines are very soft.

2. Holding the aubergines in a cloth, cut them in half lengthways and pull or scrape out the flesh into a colander. Squeeze the aubergine flesh gently to extract surplus moisture. Chop the flesh so that it still has some texture.

3. Put the aubergine flesh into a bowl and mix in the olive oil, parsley or coriander, lemon juice, cumin, onion and seasoning. Cover. It can be left in the refrigerator for as long as several hours.

4. If necessary, return the dip to room temperature a short while before serving so that it is not too cold. Make a few swirls in the surface of the dip with the back of a spoon and pour a trickle of olive oil into the whirls. Garnish with the parsley or coriander. Serve with warm pitta bread.

HUMMUS BI TAHINI Ⓥ

SERVES 2–4

This chick pea and sesame dip is just about the most well-known Middle Eastern dip. It is very simple, containing little more than those two basic ingredients, but needless to say the number of variations is enormous. Almost every cook has his or her preferred proportions of main ingredients and flavourings, so follow their lead and adjust this recipe if you feel so inclined. Serve as a first course or snack with warm pitta bread, crudités or boiled eggs, or with potatoes or other vegetables such as cauliflower, carrots, broccoli or courgettes for a main course.

1 tablespoon cumin seeds
1 × 425g (15oz) can chick peas
2 cloves garlic
6 tablespoons tahini
about 6 tablespoons lemon juice

3 tablespoons olive oil
a pinch of cayenne pepper
salt and freshly ground black pepper
olive oil and chopped parsley to garnish

1. Heat the cumin seeds in a dry, heavy frying pan for 1–2 minutes until they pop.

2. Drain the chick peas and reserve the liquid. Put the chick peas, garlic, tahini, cumin, lemon juice and oil into a blender or food processor and mix to a purée. Adjust the amount of lemon juice to taste and add enough of the reserved chick pea liquid to give a consistency similar to whipped cream. Add cayenne pepper and seasoning to taste.

3. Transfer to a serving bowl. With the back of a spoon, make swirls in the surface of the dip. Trickle oil into the swirls and garnish with the chopped parsley.

TAHINI WITH HERBS Ⓥ

SERVES 4

This is a pure tahini dip, rich and nutritious.

2–3 plump cloves garlic	leaves from a bunch of mint
1 fresh red chilli	grated zest and juice of 2 lemons
leaves from a bunch of mixed coriander	175g (6oz) tahini
and parsley	salt and freshly ground black pepper

1. With the motor running, drop the garlic and chilli into a blender or food processor, then add the herbs and lemon zest and juice and mix together well.

2. Mix in the tahini, then add enough water to mix a thick, creamy dip. Season to taste and spoon into a serving bowl.

*B*EAN DIP ⓥ

SERVES 4

For this simple dip you can use whatever type of canned beans (but not in tomato sauce) you like, or have, such as butter, flageolet, kidney, haricot, cannellini or borlotti. Accompany it with raw or lightly cooked vegetables or warm pitta bread.

3 cloves garlic
1 × 425g (15oz) can beans, drained and
   rinsed
about 4 tablespoons virgin olive oil, plus
   extra for trickling

a squeeze of lemon juice
salt and freshly ground black pepper
paprika and chopped coriander or parsley
   to serve

1. With the motor running, drop the garlic into a blender or food processor, then add the beans and oil. When well mixed, add lemon juice and seasoning to taste.

2. Turn the dip into a serving bowl and create swirls in the surface with the back of a spoon. Trickle oil into the swirls, then dust with paprika and sprinkle with the chopped coriander or parsley.

Chick Pea and Coriander Dip

SERVES 4

Good things to serve with this dip include oil-cured black olives, wedges of boiled eggs, pitta bread crisps and fingers of red pepper, courgette, cucumber, fennel or carrot. It can also be spooned on to bread and topped with lettuce, or into pitta bread.

2 tablespoons olive oil	1 × 425g (15oz) can chick peas
1 large onion, chopped	2 tablespoons lime juice
2 cloves garlic	2–3 tablespoons Greek yogurt
1 large tomato	2½ tablespoons chopped coriander
4 plump spring onions	salt and freshly ground black pepper
1 fresh red chilli	

1. Heat the oil in a frying pan, add the onion and cook for about 5 minutes, or until you have finished preparing the other ingredients.

2. Meanwhile, chop the garlic and add to the onion as it is cooking.

3. Chop the tomato. Chop the white part and some of the green part of the spring onions. Deseed and chop the chilli. Drain the chick peas, reserving a little of the liquid.

4. Transfer the contents of the frying pan to a blender or food processor and add the chick peas, chilli, lime juice, yogurt and seasoning. Mix to a nubbly purée. Add the spring onions and coriander. If the purée is not as soft as hummus, add a spoonful or two of the reserved chick pea liquid. Mix again briefly.

5. Turn into a serving bowl and stir in the tomato.

Sauce Selection

All these sauces are easy to make. They are usually cold and, rather than being an integral part of a dish, they are served as accompaniments to boiled or poached eggs and cooked or raw vegetables, or served as dips. They can also be spread on bread, tossed with pasta and stirred into rice. They can be kept in a covered container in the refrigerator for a few days.

ROUILLE

If you use red peppers bottled in oil, you may need more lemon juice. This is particularly good tossed with pasta.

2 cloves garlic	about 1 tablespoon lemon juice
2 red peppers, charred and peeled (see page 32) **or** 2 canned pimentos **or** 2 bottled red peppers, chopped	1 egg yolk
	3 tablespoons fresh breadcrumbs
	100ml (3½fl oz) olive oil
1 fresh red chilli, deseeded and chopped	salt and freshly ground black pepper

1. With the motor running, drop the garlic into a blender or food processor, followed by the peppers, chilli, lemon juice, egg yolk and breadcrumbs.

2. When all these ingredients have been added, very slowly pour in the oil, then increase the flow to a steady stream until the mixture thickens to a mayonnaise-like consistency. Add seasoning and more lemon juice, if necessary.

TARATOR

There are many versions of this Middle Eastern, Greek and Turkish sauce. For a start, the nuts may be pine nuts, walnuts or hazelnuts; or sesame seeds in the form of tahini may be used. The quickest way to make tarator is to use a blender or food processor, but if you have time you can get a better texture by pounding the garlic, nuts and bread, then gradually working in the oil.

Lebanese Tarator with Pine Nuts

1½ slices of country bread, crusts
  removed, torn
about 115g (4oz) pine nuts, chopped
about 115ml (4fl oz) olive oil

1–2 cloves garlic, crushed
about 3 tablespoons lemon juice
salt and freshly ground black pepper

1. Soak the bread in a little water until softened, then drain and squeeze dry.

2. Put the garlic, nuts and bread into a blender or food processor, mix briefly then, with the motor running, slowly pour in the oil to make a soft, thick sauce. Add lemon juice and seasoning to taste.

Turkish Tarator with Walnuts Ⓥ

1 thick slice of country bread, crusts
  removed, torn
3 cloves garlic, crushed
75g (3oz) walnuts, as fresh as possible

about 75ml (3fl oz) olive oil
lemon juice or white wine vinegar to taste
salt and freshly ground black pepper

1. Soak the bread in water until softened, then drain and squeeze dry.

2. Put the bread into a small blender or food processor with the garlic and nuts. Mix briefly then slowly pour in the oil to make a soft, thick sauce. Add lemon juice or white wine vinegar and seasoning to taste.

AILLADE Ⓥ

This nut sauce comes from Toulouse.

115g (4oz) walnuts, as fresh as possible
2 cloves garlic, crushed
75ml (3fl oz) walnut oil
75ml (3fl oz) mild olive oil

lemon juice to taste
salt and freshly ground black pepper
chopped parsley or chives to serve

---

1. Preheat the grill. Lightly toast the nuts, then drop into a blender or food processor, add the garlic and mix briefly.

2. With the motor running, slowly pour in the oils.

3. Add lemon juice and seasoning to taste, and about 2 tablespoons water – enough to give a light cream.

4. Serve sprinkled with the parsley or chives.

YOGURT WITH CUCUMBER AND MINT

SERVES 4

It is important to use proper Greek yogurt for this dish. If you are making the recipe in advance and chilling it before serving, the cucumber should be sprinkled with salt and left for about one hour to remove surplus water, otherwise the dish will be watery when it is served. However, if you are going to serve the dish straightaway this won't be necessary; but you will need to have well-chilled yogurt, and preferably a 'fridge-cold cucumber or at least one that is not warm.

½ cucumber
a squeeze of lemon juice
1 tablespoon chopped mint

1 clove garlic, crushed (optional)
150ml (5fl oz) Greek yogurt, chilled
salt and freshly ground black pepper

1. Peel the cucumber, cut in half lengthways and scoop out of the seeds. Either finely chop or thinly slice the cucumber and toss with a small squeeze of lemon juice.

2. Mix the cucumber, mint, and garlic, if liked, into the yogurt and season to taste. Serve straightaway.

GRILLED ASPARAGUS WITH SHAVED PARMESAN

SERVES 2

This is a simple yet special dish. I know that asparagus, like so many other foods, is now available all year round, but for me no other asparagus beats the really fresh green of the English ones that are available for a short spell in early summer. I therefore try to make the most of them while I have the chance. This is an ideal way of achieving this. Grilling intensifies the flavour of the asparagus so (hopefully) your taste buds will have the impression that they have had more than they actually have.

virgin olive oil

about 300g (10oz) slim asparagus spears

a piece of Parmesan for shaving

salt and freshly ground black pepper

1. Preheat the grill or a ridged cast-iron pan. Tip a little oil over the bottom of a shallow dish, add the asparagus, trickle a little more oil over the spears and turn them over so they are coated.

2. Cook the asparagus under the grill or in the pan, turning as necessary (using tongs is the easiest way), until the spears are tender and flecked with brown.

3. Transfer to a warm plate, season and shave Parmesan over the asparagus. Serve straightaway.

POTATOES WITH AÏOLI

SERVES 4–6

The number of garlic cloves in this dish can be adjusted according to taste. If you have time, try baking the garlic cloves wrapped in foil, or grilling them, until they are soft to get a softer, more smoky-flavoured sauce. The sauce can be made in a blender – with the motor running, drop the garlic into the goblet, then add the egg yolk and mix briefly. Very slowly pour in the oil, as when making mayonnaise, until the sauce is thick. Add lemon juice and seasoning to taste. The potatoes can be peeled or unpeeled.

450g (1lb) new potatoes, or waxy
  potatoes
about 4 cloves garlic
1 egg yolk

150ml (5fl oz) olive oil
juice of ½ lemon
salt and freshly ground black pepper
chopped parsley to serve

---

1. Bring a saucepan of water to the boil. If the potatoes are large, cut them into quarters or eighths, depending on size. Add to the boiling water and boil for 8–10 minutes until tender.

2. Meanwhile, using a pestle and mortar, crush the garlic with a pinch of salt, then mix in the egg yolk. Add the oil very slowly at first, then in a slow, steady stream, mixing constantly, as when making mayonnaise. Add the lemon juice and season to taste.

3. Drain the potatoes and toss with the alioli. Sprinkle with the chopped parsley and serve.

MUSHROOMS A LA GREQUE Ⓥ

SERVES 4

Despite what the name might suggest, this is not a Greek dish, but a French one. In the sixties and seventies mushrooms *à la Greque*, served cold, was a popular way of giving white button mushrooms some character, but I always felt they were a bit slimy to eat, and that they didn't add anything to the dish. Today, I use brown cap button mushrooms (button mushrooms are best as they have to withstand boiling without disintegrating) because they contribute to the flavour and are nicer to eat. I always make enough hot mushrooms for four, even if only two of us are going to eat them, and leave half to cool, then keep them, covered, in a cool place (preferably not the refrigerator) overnight for a delicious starter the next day.

3 tablespoons virgin oil

1 red onion, finely chopped

1 clove garlic, crushed

1 tablespoon coriander seeds, coarsely crushed

450g (1lb) brown cap button mushrooms or larger mushrooms, broken into large pieces

about 1 tablespoon lemon juice

1 tablespoon sherry vinegar

1 bay leaf

a pinch of brown sugar

225ml (8fl oz) passata

1 tablespoon chopped coriander

salt and freshly ground black pepper

fresh, firm bread to serve

1. Heat the oil in a frying pan, add the red onion and garlic and cook for about 5 minutes. Add the coriander seeds and heat for about 30 seconds until fragrant.

2. Add all the remaining ingredients, except the bread, and boil for 5–6 minutes.

3. Using a slotted spoon, scoop the mushrooms out into a bowl. Boil the sauce hard until reduced by half. Adjust the vinegar, lemon juice and sugar, if necessary, then stir into the mushrooms. Serve with firm bread.

GREEK BEACH GRILL

SERVES 2

During a short, slow stroll before going back to our rented house to prepare supper, the delicious smell of a barbecue caught our nostrils and we wandered on, ever more quickly, towards the source of the tantalising aroma until we came across a simple taverna by the beach. The food smelt so good we couldn't resist seeing if it also tasted good. It did. So we didn't have to bother to make our own supper. The only trouble was, we had to walk home afterwards. Although I have given instructions for cooking the Grill under a grill, it would have a more authentic taste if cooked on a barbecue, when you have time. The Grill can be served warm or left to cool.

---

1 fresh red pepper
225g (8oz) small courgettes
1 clove garlic
2 tablespoons virgin olive oil, plus extra
   for brushing

1 tablespoon lemon juice
1–1½ tablespoons chopped mint
salt and freshly ground black pepper
50g (2oz) feta cheese to serve

---

1. Preheat the grill. Cut the pepper into quarters and thickly slice the courgettes. Put the pepper, skin-side up, and courgettes on the grill rack and brush them with oil. Grill until the skin of the pepper is charred and blistered, and the courgettes are tender and both sides of the slices are browned. Remove the vegetables from the grill rack as they are done.

2. Meanwhile, crush the garlic then mix it with the 2 tablespoons oil, lemon juice and seasoning.

3. When the courgettes are ready, mix the slices with the dressing and mint.

4. When the pepper is ready, leave until cool enough to handle then peel off the skin. Cut the pepper into strips and add to the courgettes.

5. Leave the vegetables to cool or serve warm; either way, crumble the cheese over them just before serving.

SPICED AUBERGINES WITH TOMATO SAUCE Ⓥ

SERVES 4

This is different from most aubergine and tomato sauce recipes in that the aubergines are fried until crisp and brown, then added to the sauce for just a brief time rather than being stewed in it. Serve with robust bread such as sourdough or rye, accompanied by bowls of oil-cured black olives and cool Greek yogurt. The dish is also good cold.

3 small aubergines
6 tablespoons olive oil
2 onions, finely chopped
2 cloves garlic
6 well-flavoured tomatoes
1 teaspoon ground allspice

1 teaspoon ground cumin
a pinch of cayenne pepper
1½ tablespoons chopped coriander
1½ tablespoons chopped mint
salt and freshly ground black pepper
mint leaves to garnish

1. Cut the aubergines into 1.25cm (½ inch) cubes. Set aside.

2. Heat half the oil in a frying pan, add the onion and cook until golden and soft.

3. Meanwhile, crush the garlic and chop the tomatoes (you can also peel them if you like). Stir the garlic, spices, coriander, mint, tomatoes and seasoning into the onion and cook gently for 5–10 minutes, stirring occasionally.

4. Heat the remaining oil in a large frying pan, add the aubergines and stir-fry until tender and golden. Drain on paper towels and stir into the tomato mixture, then serve garnished with the mint leaves.

PEPERONATA ⓥ

SERVES 2–3 *as a first course or light meal, 4 as an accompaniment*

Peperonata is good warm or cold, with plenty of good bread, for a first course or for a light lunch, when it could be served cold as part of a selection of salads. It also partners plainly cooked eggs, can be tossed with pasta, stirred into rice, spread on pizzas, used as a topping for toast or firm bread or spooned into rolls.

3 tablespoons virgin olive oil
1 large onion, thinly sliced
2 large red peppers
1 large yellow pepper
2 cloves garlic
4 plum tomatoes

1 tablespoon balsamic vinegar
1 tablespoon chopped parsley or basil
4–6 black olives, preferably oil-cured
   (optional)
salt and freshly ground black pepper

1. Heat the oil in a heavy-based frying pan, add the onion and cook.

2. Meanwhile, thickly slice the peppers lengthways. Crush the garlic.

3. Add the peppers and garlic to the pan and cook, stirring occasionally, until the peppers are beginning to soften.

4. While the peppers are cooking, seed and quarter the tomatoes

5. Stir the tomatoes into the peppers and cook gently for about 10 minutes. Stir in the vinegar, parsley or basil, the olives if liked, and seasoning.

Ratatouille with Mozzarella Crostini

SERVES 4

Many purists say that the vegetables for ratatouille should be fried separately before being brought together for the final simmering in the sauce, but when I'm in a hurry there is no time for such refinements so I simply cook them all at once. To make more of a meal of ratatouille, I serve it with cheese-topped French bread; I like to use a granary baguette, or, for a change, Italian ciabatta, which is more chewy and filling. Herb breads are also good. Ratatouille makes a delicious filling for omelettes or a base for poached, soft-boiled or scrambled eggs.

2 tablespoons olive oil
3 cloves garlic
1 aubergine, chopped
2 red peppers or 1 red pepper and
  1 yellow pepper
2 courgettes, chopped

1 medium baguette
4 large, ripe, well-flavoured tomatoes
1 tablespoon chopped parsley
2 tablespoons chopped basil
225g (8oz) mozzarella cheese
salt and freshly ground black pepper

1. Preheat the grill. Heat the oil in a large, preferably non-stick, frying pan, and fry the garlic, aubergine, peppers and courgettes for about 10 minutes until beginning to soften.

2. Meanwhile, cut the bread into four even lengths, then cut each piece in half lengthways and toast. Chop the tomatoes.

3. Add the tomatoes, herbs and seasoning to the vegetables and simmer gently until the vegetables are tender and there is no free liquid.

4. While the vegetables are cooking, grate the mozzarella, cover the cut sides of the bread with it and grill until golden. Serve with the ratatouille.

COURGETTES WITH PESTO, CHEESE AND ALMONDS

SERVES 2

Instead of goat's cheese you could use grated mozzarella or Gruyère cheese, or soft cheese.

4 courgettes	about 2 tablespoons flaked almonds
olive oil for brushing	1 tablespoon chopped tarragon (optional)
75g (3oz) soft goat's cheese	black pepper
2 tablespoons pesto	

1. Preheat the grill. Halve the courgettes lengthways, brush with the olive oil and place, cut-side down, on the grill pan. Grill until lightly browned.

2. Thinly slice the cheese.

3. Turn the courgettes over and spread the pesto over the cut sides. Cover them with slices of goat's cheese, grind black pepper over them and scatter with the almonds. Return to the grill until their tops are lightly browned.

4. Sprinkle with the tarragon, if liked, and serve.

*F*ALAFEL

SERVES 4

*F*alafel can be served in split pitta bread, with shredded lettuce and chopped tomatoes, and topped with tahini diluted with lemon juice and water, or yogurt mixed with a little lemon juice. Alternatively, they can be served with a thin mayonnaise or light tomato sauce or salsa like the one below.

1–2 cloves garlic

1 × 425g (15oz) can chick peas, drained

1 teaspoon ground cumin

leaves and fine stems from a bunch of parsley

leaves and fine stems from a bunch of coriander

a small pinch of cayenne pepper

1 onion, very finely chopped

1 canned or bottled red pepper (sometimes labelled pimento when canned), finely chopped (optional)

1 egg, beaten

olive oil for frying

salt and freshly ground black pepper

1. With the motor running, drop the garlic into a blender or food processor, then add the chick peas, ground cumin, parsley, coriander and cayenne and mix to a coarse purée.

2. Transfer to a bowl and stir in all the remaining ingredients except the oil.

3. Divide the chick pea mixture into 12 small balls and flatten them into cakes.

4. Fry the falafel in oil over a moderate heat for 4–5 minutes a side until brown and crisp. Remove with a fish slice and drain on paper towels. Serve hot.

Tomato and Red Pepper Sauce

Mix 2 chopped well-flavoured ridged tomatoes, 1 clove garlic, ½ chopped red onion and 1 chopped red pepper to a nubbly sauce in a blender or food processor; don't overdo it. Add a dash of red wine vinegar, if liked. Chopped herbs can be added when this is not being served with falafel.

MOROCCAN AUBERGINE BRIOUTS

SERVES 4 *for a first course (makes 8 pastries)*

Briouts are the same as Tunisian *briks* (see page 40) and Turkish *boreks* (see page 39). In this recipe, the crisp, delicate pastry encloses a spicy, moist filling to make a light and extremely 'moreish' starter or snack. Don't be put off by the length of the method – it is just because I have given very precise directions on how to slice and quarter the aubergine, but the recipe is not difficult or time-consuming.

1 clove garlic

4 tablespoons olive oil, plus extra for brushing the pastries, if necessary

1 teaspoon ground cumin

a pinch of paprika

2 small aubergines, each weighing about 225g (8oz)

4 tablespoons Greek yogurt

2 tablespoons chopped coriander

2 sheets of filo pastry

sesame oil for brushing (optional)

3 teaspoons sesame seeds

salt and freshly ground black pepper

chilled Greek yogurt to serve (optional)

1. Preheat the oven to 200°C/400°F/Gas Mark 6. Preheat the grill.

2. Crush the garlic, then mix with the 4 tablespoons olive oil, cumin and paprika. Cut each aubergine in half lengthways. Put, cut-side down, on the work surface, then cut across the aubergines into very thin slices. Holding the slices in the shape of the aubergine, cut each aubergine half lengthways in half again. Spread out in a single layer on a baking sheet and brush with the spiced oil. Grill for about 3 minutes a side until beginning to brown; brush the second side of the slices with oil when you turn them over.

3. Tip the aubergine into a large bowl and mix with the yogurt and coriander. Season to taste.

4. Lay out one filo sheet on the work surface (keep the other sheet covered) and brush with some of the spiced oil. Cut into 4 lengthways. Put 2 tablespoons of the aubergine mixture about 5 cm (2 inches) from one short end. Fold a corner of the short side over the aubergine mixture to make a triangle. Fold the triangle over and over along the length of the strip. Put on the baking sheet. Repeat with the remaining pastry and aubergine mixture. Brush the pastries with sesame oil, if liked (otherwise use olive oil), and sprinkle with the sesame seeds.

5. Bake for 10–12 minutes until brown and crisp and serve with chilled Greek yogurt, if liked.

CHEESE BOREKS

MAKES 10–12 pastries

These are probably the most popular of the variously filled Turkish pastries, and are the easiest and quickest to make because the filling does not require any preparation. They are very difficult to resist and will disappear surprisingly soon, so when you have time make double the recipe.

75g (3oz) feta or goat's cheese, crumbled	about 3 sheets of filo pastry
25g (1oz) curd cheese	olive oil and melted butter for brushing
2 tablespoons chopped mixed parsley and dill	freshly ground black pepper

1. Preheat the oven to 375°C/190°F/Gas Mark 5.

2. Mash the feta or goat's cheese with a fork, then mix in the curd cheese, herbs and pepper.

3. With the sheets of filo pastry in a stack, cut lengthways into strips about 7.5cm (4 inches) wide. Lay one strip on the work surface and brush with melted butter and oil; cover the remaining strips with a damp tea towel to prevent them from drying out.

4. Put a heaped teaspoon of the filling near the end of the pastry strip, shaping it into a small sausage shape parallel to the edge. Fold the sides of the pastry over the filling, then neatly roll up the strip. Place on a baking sheet. Repeat with the remaining pastry and cheese. Brush the pastries with butter and oil.

5. Bake for about 10 minutes until crisp and golden. Serve warm.

BRIKS A L'OEUF

SERVES 4

These light, crisp Tunisian pastries look very innocent but eating them without getting egg on your face, literally, is quite an art – one that it is no hardship to master. Eat the *briks* immediately they are served. To be truly authentic, gossamer-thin Tunisian *warka* (also spelt *ouarka*) pastry should be used, but it is very difficult to make and cannot be bought; Chinese spring roll wrappers, or filo pastry, make a satisfactory alternative. Unconventional, perhaps, but the wrappers can be spread with pesto or black olive paste or the eggs can be topped with finely grated Parmesan cheese sprinkled or a small knob of garlic butter.

---

4 Chinese spring roll wrappers
2 tablespoons very finely chopped spring
  onion
2 tablespoons finely chopped coriander
  or parsley

4 small eggs
1 egg white, lightly beaten
olive oil for frying
salt and freshly ground black pepper

---

1. Spread out the spring roll wrappers and put 2 teaspoons each of spring onion and coriander or parsley on one half of each one. Break an egg over each portion of filling. Season the eggs. Fold over the wrapper to cover the filling and firmly seal the edges with egg white, giving the edges a double fold for extra security.

2. Heat a 2.5cm (1 inch) depth of oil in a large frying pan until very hot but not smoking and slide in the *briks*. Baste their tops with hot oil and fry quickly until the undersides are browned. Turn the *briks* over and fry their other sides.

3. Use a fish slice to transfer the *briks* to paper towels to drain briefly, then serve straightaway.

EGG AND BASIL MAYONNAISE SANDWICHES

MAKES 2 rounds

Butter is quite unnecessary for these sandwiches, and this is one instance where firm bread is wrong. These are my standard egg sandwiches and after I had served them to a member of a local cricket team, he was so enthusiastic that he asked the ladies who make the cricket teas if they would make theirs like mine – a request that was met with an icy riposte to the effect that they did not have enough basil growing in their gardens to make enough sandwiches for the 35 or so people for whom they catered, and did he know how much it would cost to buy sufficient of the herb? Instead of mixing the basil into the mayonnaise in a blender, you could chop it finely and stir it in; the results are different and it is a matter of preference which is preferred.

4 eggs, at room temperature
2–3 basil leaves
about 4 tablespoons mayonnaise

4 slices of very fresh wholemeal bread
salt and freshly ground black pepper

1. Bring a small saucepan of water to the boil, add the eggs and simmer for about 4–4½ minutes until the white is set but the yolk is still creamy.

2. Meanwhile, put the basil leaves and the mayonnaise into a blender and mix together. Taste, and add more basil if necessary.

3. Drain the eggs and rinse under running cold water. Peel and chop the eggs.

4. Spread the basil mayonnaise over the bread and top 2 slices with egg. Season.

5. Top the slices with the remaining bread, cut in half and eat.

MOZZARELLA AND BREAD SKEWERS

SERVES 4

Instead of the quickly made tomato and basil sauce, which is prepared in much the same way as pesto, the skewers can be served with Red and Yellow Pepper Relish (see page 63), Green Sauce (see page 61) or the dressing for the Garlic Bread Salad made with basil, rather than parsley (see page 75). The skewers can be cooked on a barbecue.

12 slices from an Italian or French loaf, 1.25cm (½ inch) thick
8 slices of mozzarella, about 6mm–1.25cm (¼–½ inches) thick
olive oil for brushing
salt and freshly ground black pepper

Tomato and Basil Sauce
3 cloves garlic
40g (1½oz) basil leaves

75g (3oz) blanched almonds, coarsely chopped
350g (12oz) well-flavoured tomatoes, peeled, seeded and coarsely chopped
75ml (3fl oz) virgin olive oil
50g (2oz) pecorino or Parmesan cheese, freshly grated
2–3 teaspoons sun-dried tomato paste (optional)

1. To make the sauce, drop the garlic into a small blender while the motor is running, then add the basil. When almost mixed to a paste, add the almonds, mix briefly then add the tomatoes. When pulpy, slowly pour in the oil. Add the cheese and seasoning. Mix briefly, then taste to see if sun-dried tomato paste is necessary. Set aside.

2. Preheat the grill. Thread 3 slices of bread and 2 slices of mozzarella alternately on to each of 4 skewers, beginning and ending with bread and packing the slices together tightly.

3. Brush the bread and cheese with oil and season them.

4. Grill until the bread is toasted and the cheese is beginning to melt. Serve straightaway accompanied by the sauce.

MUSHROOM AND BREAD SPEDIENI Ⓥ

SERVES 2

Spedieni are an Italian vegetarian version of kebabs. The bread, which becomes impregnated with the garlicky-herby oil and the flavour of mushrooms, should be about the same diameter as the mushrooms, certainly no smaller. Serve on lightly dressed rocket or spinach. These skewers can be cooked on a barbecue.

---

eight 2cm (¾ inch) thick slices of firm,
   baguette-style bread
2 cloves garlic
3 tablespoons virgin olive oil
1 tablespoon finely chopped rosemary

1 teaspoon finely chopped sage
6 chestnut, shiitake or oyster mushrooms
   about 6cm (2½ inches) in diameter,
   stalks removed
salt and freshly ground black pepper

---

1. Preheat the grill to moderate. Toast the bread slowly so the slices become dry and crisp, then increase the heat to normal toasting temperature.

2. Meanwhile, finely chop the garlic and mix with the oil, rosemary, sage and seasoning. Brush some over the mushrooms, pressing the garlic and herbs into their undersides.

3. Brush the bread with the remaining oil mixture, then thread alternately with the mushrooms on to 2 skewers, beginning and ending with a slice of bread.

4. Lightly grill the skewers for 3–5 minutes, turning frequently, until golden.

BRUSCHETTA WITH TOMATOES, OLIVES AND BASIL Ⓥ

MAKES 4

I have taken the simple bruschetta – which authentically is no more than very ripe, tasty tomatoes crushed on to bread and dressed with very good, rich olive oil – a few steps further to make it well-flavoured without the luscious tomatoes and expensive oil, and slightly more substantial. If you have the oven on, the bread can be baked at about 200°C/400°F/Gas Mark 6, or on the top shelf of an oven at 180°C/350°F/Gas Mark 4, or the lowest shelf of an oven at 220°C/425°F/Gas Mark 7, for 5–10 minutes.

4 well-flavoured ripe tomatoes, seeded and chopped
2 cloves garlic, chopped
leaves from about 5 sprigs of basil, chopped

65g (2½oz) oil-cured black olives, stones removed, chopped
2 tablespoons extra virgin olive oil
four 1.25cm (½ inch) thick slices of ciabatta
salt and freshly ground black pepper

1. Preheat the grill. Stir together the tomatoes, garlic, basil, olives, oil and seasoning. Set aside.

2. Toast the bread until lightly browned on both sides. Cover with the tomato mixture and serve.

Sun-dried Tomato,
Cheese and Basil Crostini

Serves 3–4

Eat these in your fingers, or serve on a crisp mixed salad for a snack or light meal.

1 medium Granary or wholemeal
  baguette
1 plump clove garlic, halved lengthways
oil from sun-dried tomatoes or olive oil
  for brushing
about 50g (2oz) sun-dried tomatoes in oil

40–50g (1½–2oz) mozzarella cheese
50g (2oz) stoned black olives
2 tablespoons chopped basil
black pepper
basil leaves to garnish

1. Preheat the grill. Cut the loaf into 12 slices, rub with the cut sides of the garlic and brush with the oil from the sun-dried tomatoes, or olive oil. Toast on both sides.

2. Meanwhile, slice the sun-dried tomatoes, grate the mozzarella and quarter the olives.

3. Top the bread with the sun-dried tomatoes and olives. Grind pepper over and trickle over a little of the oil from the tomatoes. Add the basil followed by the mozzarella.

4. Return to the grill until the cheese is golden and bubbling. Serve with the basil leaves scattered over.

GOAT'S CHEESE ON CIABATTA

SERVES 2–4

Traditional British cheese on toast was one of my favourite snacks. But now that there is a much wider choice of foods readily available, it has been pushed aside in favour of lightly toasted ciabatta and goat's cheese. In this recipe I have expanded slightly upon simple cheese on bread to make it more of a light meal than just a snack.

1 teaspoon black olive paste
1 teaspoon chopped thyme
½ clove garlic, chopped
3 tablespoons olive oil
2 teaspoons white wine vinegar
1 ciabatta loaf

3 well-flavoured tomatoes
225g (8oz) log of goat's cheese
8 basil leaves
black pepper
salad leaves to serve

1. Preheat the grill.

2. Whisk together the black olive paste, thyme, garlic, oil, vinegar and pepper.

3. Cut the loaf in half horizontally, then cut each piece in half vertically. Brush some of the dressing over the cut sides of the bread, then toast lightly on those sides.

4. Meanwhile, slice the tomatoes and cut the cheese into 12 slices.

5. Cover the cut sides of the bread with the tomatoes, scatter with the basil, then arrange the cheese on top. Grind black pepper over the cheese and put under the grill until the cheese is browned.

6. Meanwhile, put salad leaves on each plate and trickle over the remaining dressing. Add a piece of bread to each plate and serve.

TOASTED AUBERGINE, TOMATO AND CHEESE SANDWICH

SERVES 2

This is a knife and fork main course sandwich.

2 cloves garlic, finely chopped
75ml (3fl oz) olive oil
3 small aubergines (or 2 slightly larger
   ones), total weight about 350g (12oz)
1 large, well-flavoured tomato

four 1.25cm (½ inch) thick diagonal slices
   of firm bread
about 115g (4oz) fontina cheese
4 tablespoons chopped basil
salt and freshly ground black pepper

1. Preheat the grill. Finely chop the garlic and mix with the oil. Cut the aubergines lengthways into 3. Brush both sides with some of the oil.

2. Grill the aubergines for about 5–7 minutes until soft and slightly charred.

3. While the aubergine is cooking, slice the tomato. Brush both sides of the bread and tomato slices with the remaining oil. Add to the grill rack and grill for 1 minute a side, until the bread is golden and the tomatoes begin to soften.

4. Set 2 slices of bread aside. Cover the remaining bread with the aubergine, then fontina, then tomato and basil. Season and return to the grill for about 1 minute until the cheese begins to melt.

5. Top with the remaining bread and serve.

47

PITTA BREAD WITH AVOCADO SALAD Ⓥ

SERVES 2

I always keep some pitta breads in the freezer as they can so easily be made into a quick snack, packed lunch or even a light meal, depending on what I have available to use as a filling. All sorts of combinations of hot and cold, freshly prepared or leftover ingredients can be popped into the open mouth of a pitta bread that has had a brief sojurn under a hot grill – Ratatouille (see page 35), Caponata (see page 86), the egg dishes on pages 59–61 and many of the salads, to name but a few. I only ever eat this avocado salad in a pitta bread because I love it this way – on its own it leaves me cold. However, I am in a minority of one - other people enjoy it as much out of the bread as in it.

1 large ripe avocado, finely chopped	1 tablespoon lime juice
1 ripe well-flavoured tomato, finely chopped	2 tablespoons chopped coriander
	a dash of Tabasco sauce
1 red onion, finely chopped	2 pitta breads
1 red pepper, finely chopped	salt and freshly ground black pepper
2 cloves garlic, finely chopped	lettuce leaves
2 tablespoons virgin olive oil	

1. Preheat the grill. Mix together the avocado, tomato, red onion, red pepper, garlic, olive oil, lime juice, coriander, Tabasco sauce and seasoning.

2. Toast the pitta breads until they puff up.

3. Split the pitta breads, line with lettuce leaves and spoon in the avocado salad.

PAN BAGNAT

SERVES 2–4

Pan bagnat is a *provençal* salad roll *par excellence* and ideal for taking on picnics. Around Nice, hard loaves about 20cm (8 inches) long are baked especially for this dish. The filled loaves are traditionally wrapped firmly and left with a weight on top for at least 2 hours so that the juices soak into the bread and the flavours meld, but when softer bread is used, the *Pan bagnat* can be eaten straightaway.

The choice of salad ingredients usually encompasses some if not all of the following: cucumber, onion, black olives, radishes, red peppers, tomatoes, garlic, lettuce and vinaigrette dressing, and perhaps hard-boiled egg or anchovies. I have made a few changes for this version here, but kept the regional feel. Feel free to make what adjustments or additions you like.

3 tablespoons virgin olive oil

1 tablespoon white wine vinegar

1 clove garlic, finely chopped

2 tablespoons chopped parsley

2 small flat round loaves

4 lettuce leaves

1 small red pepper, thinly sliced

2 spring onions, white and some green part finely chopped

2–3 artichoke hearts in oil, chopped

½ cucumber, peeled, deseeded and diced

1 well-flavoured ridged tomato, sliced

8 black olives, preferably oil-cured, stones removed and chopped

1½ tablespoons pine nuts, toasted if liked

50g (2oz) mozzarella cheese, grated

salt and freshly ground black pepper

1. Whisk together the oil, vinegar, garlic, parsley and seasoning. Cut the loaves in half and scoop out the soft crumbs.

2. Brush the insides of the halves with some of the dressing. Line 2 of the halves with 2 of the lettuce leaves. Layer the vegetables, olives, nuts and mozzarella in these halves. Sprinkle generously with the remaining dressing and put the remaining lettuce leaves on top.

3. Cover with the top halves of the loaves and press firmly together.

*F*RIED HALOUMI CHEESE

SERVES 2

This is a good dish to make when you are doing a main course, such as Spanish Chick peas with Spinach (see page 115), or dessert that requires a certain amount of preparation, as the cheese can be left to marinate in the oil while you get on with the rest of the meal. Then, when you are ready to eat, all you have to do is quickly fry the cheese and serve it.

---

2 teaspoons chopped marjoram or thyme
2 tablespoons olive oil
115g (4oz) haloumi cheese, cut into 4
   slices

freshly ground black pepper
capers, preferably salt-cured, chopped if
   large, or lemon wedges to serve
   (optional)

---

1. Mix the marjoram or thyme and pepper into the oil. Lay the cheese slices in a shallow dish and pour the oil mixture over them. Turn the cheese over. Leave for as long as possible – up to 1 hour.

2. Pour the oil from the dish into a frying pan and heat. Add the cheese slices and fry for 1–2 minutes until browned.

3. Transfer to warm plates, scatter with capers, if liked, and pour over the oil from the pan. Serve with lemon wedges, if liked.

*F*RIED CHEESE, OLIVES AND SUN-DRIED TOMATOES

SERVES 2–3

This is a quick, tasty snack, or impromptu first course.

2 tablespoons virgin olive oil
8 oil-cured black olives, stoned and sliced
225g (8oz) haloumi cheese, cubed
2 halves of sun-dried tomato in oil,
   drained and sliced

freshly ground black pepper
small basil leaves, or chopped parsley,
   coriander or oregano to garnish
lemon wedges and good bread to serve

1. Heat the oil in a frying pan over a low heat. Add the olives, cheese and sun-dried tomatoes and fry, stirring occasionally, until the cheese is lightly browned.

2. Season with pepper and scatter with your chosen herb. Serve with lemon wedges and good bread.

Baked Cheesey Tomatoes

Serves 2

If preferred, instead of the goat's cheese you could use a soft cheese flavoured with herbs and garlic or pepper. If you cook the tomatoes in one shallow dish, use a fish slice to transfer them carefully to warm plates.

2 large tomatoes	2 teaspoons finely chopped basil
40g (1½oz) mozzarella cheese	salt and freshly ground black pepper
50g (2oz) soft goat's cheese	country bread to serve

1. Preheat the oven to 180°C/350°F/Gas Mark 4.

2. Cut a thin slice off the top of each tomato. Using a teaspoon, scoop out the seeds and most of the flesh from the tomatoes, taking care not to pierce the skins. Reserve the juice from the tomatoes. Put the tomato shells in individual gratin dishes or a shallow baking dish.

3. Grate the mozzarella into a bowl then mix in the goat's cheese, basil and seasoning. Add enough of the tomato juice to give a thick, creamy consistency. Divide between the tomato shells.

4. Bake for about 20 minutes until the cheese is melted and golden and the tomatoes softened slightly. Serve with country bread.

GRILLED GOAT'S CHEESE IN VINE LEAVES

SERVES 4

It goes without saying that these are best grilled over a barbecue (cook them while it is heating up – when it is completely hot the heat is too fierce). I like to rub the bread that accompanies the cheese with a cut garlic clove before warming it.

8 vine leaves about 15cm (6 inches) across	2 tablespoons chopped mixed herbs such as parsley, chives, oregano and thyme
olive oil for brushing	black pepper
450g (1lb) goat's cheese, cut into 50g (2oz) pieces	virgin olive oil (optional) and warm country or French bread to serve

1. Preheat the grill.

2. Rinse the vine leaves but do not dry them; the water will prevent them scorching. Oil the underside of each leaf and put a piece of cheese on top. Brush the cheese with oil and sprinkle with the herbs. Grind black pepper over then fold over the leaves to enclose the cheese. Tuck the stalks in to secure the packages.

3. Put, folded side down, under a hot grill for about 2 minutes until the cheese has softened and the leaves are lightly charred.

4. Open the packages and serve immediately with virgin olive oil trickled over them, if liked, accompanied by warm country or French bread.

PIPERADE

SERVES 4

The proportions of the vegetables in the mixture and the ratio of vegetables to eggs can be adjusted.

2 tablespoons virgin olive oil	450g (1lb) very ripe, well-flavoured
1 onion, chopped	tomatoes
2 cloves garlic	4 eggs
2 red peppers	salt and freshly ground black pepper
1 yellow or green pepper	

1. Heat the oil in a large, heavy frying pan, add the onion and fry until softened but not coloured.

2. Meanwhile, chop the garlic and add to the pan to cook with the onion.

3. While the onion and garlic are cooking, slice the peppers and chop the tomatoes. Stir into the onion and simmer gently for about 15 minutes, stirring occasionally, until lightly thickened.

4. Beat and season the eggs then stir into the pan and cook over a low heat, stirring gently, until the eggs begin to thicken. Immediately remove from the heat and serve.

Huevos a la Flamenca

SERVES 2–4

Spanish *mélange* of vegetables that can be varied to suit individual tastes, or what is seasonally available; broad beans and/or asparagus can be added, for example. The eggs can be topped with grated cheese for a more filling and savoury dish; meat eaters could add some spicy chorizo sausage.

2 tablespoons olive oil	4 large well-flavoured tomatoes
1 onion, chopped	75g (3oz) thawed frozen peas
1 leek	2 tablespoons chopped parsley
2 cloves garlic	4 eggs
115g (4oz) green beans	salt and paprika

1. Heat the oil in a frying pan, add the onion and fry until transparent.

2. Meanwhile, thinly slice the leek and chop the garlic. Add both to the pan while the onion is cooking.

3. While those vegetables are cooking, bring a saucepan of water to the boil. Cut the beans into 2.5cm (1 inch) lengths and chop the tomatoes.

4. Add the tomatoes, peas and parsley to the frying pan and simmer for about 5 minutes, stirring occasionally.

5. Cook the beans in the boiling water for 5 minutes. Drain well and add to the frying pan. Cook for 5 minutes.

6. Season with salt and paprika, then make 4 deep depressions in the vegetable mixture. Break an egg into each depression, cover the pan and cook gently until the eggs are cooked to your liking.

Chakchouka

SERVES 2–4

This makes a tasty first course for four people or a satisfying light meal for two, if accompanied by good bread and a crisp salad. I have also enjoyed it spooned into split pitta bread.

3 tablespoons olive oil
1 Spanish onion, thinly sliced
2 cloves garlic
2 red peppers
1–2 fresh red chillies
675g (1½lb) well-flavoured tomatoes

about 2 teaspoons sun-dried tomato paste or a pinch of sugar (optional)
4 eggs
salt and freshly ground black pepper
chopped parsley to garnish (optional)

1. Heat the oil in a large, deep frying pan, add the onion and cook until it is soft and beginning to colour.

2. Meanwhile, chop the garlic and add to the onion while it is cooking.

3. Thinly slice the peppers and chop the chillies. Add to the softened onion and cook, stirring occasionally until almost softened.

4. While the peppers are cooking, chop the tomatoes. Stir into the pan and cook for a further 8 minutes or so until the vegetables are soft but not reduced to a mush.

5. Season and, if the flavour needs boosting or sweetening, add sun-dried tomato paste or a pinch of sugar.

6. Make 4 deep depressions in the vegetable mixture, break an egg into each, cover the pan and cook gently until the eggs are set to the preferred degree, basting once or twice with the cooking juices. Garnish with the chopped parsley, if liked.

PASTA FRITTATA WITH GOAT'S CHEESE AND TOMATO

SERVES 4

Making a frittata is a wonderful way to use leftover pasta, whether plain or dressed – the other ingredients add to the savour of the cooked dish. You can also add precooked or specially cooked vegetables, grated cheese, herbs, sun-dried tomatoes or whatever other flavourings you fancy. Or make the frittata more creamy by adding soft cheese, perhaps with garlic and herbs. If cooking pasta to make the frittata, do it for slightly less time than usual. For this recipe I use angel hair (capelletti) but large spaghetti or other types of pasta could be used.

4 eggs	2 well-flavoured tomatoes
115g (4oz) cooked angel hair pasta	2 teaspoons balsamic vinegar
2 cloves garlic, finely chopped	1 tablespoon chopped basil
2 tablespoons chopped parsley	1½ tablespoons freshly grated Parmesan
1½ tablespoons olive oil	cheese
75g (3oz) soft goat's cheese	salt and freshly ground black pepper

1. Lightly beat the eggs, then stir in the pasta, garlic, parsley and seasoning.

2. Heat the oil in a frying pan, pour in the egg mixture and spread it out evenly. Cook over a medium heat for about 10 minutes until most of the mixture is set, but the top is still creamy.

3. Meanwhile, preheat the grill. Finely chop the goat's cheese. Chop the tomatoes and mix with the vinegar, basil and seasoning.

4. Scatter the goat's cheese over the frittata and put under the grill until golden.

5. Sprinkle the Parmesan over the top of the frittata and serve in wedges with the tomatoes.

Note:
If you are using raw pasta, cook 50g (2oz) for 1–2 minutes if fresh, 3–4 minutes if dried.

Artichoke Frittata

Serves 4

Fresh globe artichokes are a summery food, but for speed and without comprising too much on flavour I use artichokes that have been grown in a sunny place such as Italy, then packed in olive oil. Canned artichokes are not a good substitute. I like my frittate slightly moist but as I also like this one with a grilled cheese topping, I leave the egg mixture fairly moist and make sure the grill is really hot, then just flash the pan under it. Alternatively, the grilling can be omitted; simply sprinkle the remaining Parmesan cheese over the top of the frittata.

2 tablespoons olive oil
1 large onion, chopped
300g (10oz) jar artichokes in oil
50g (2oz) Parmesan cheese

6 eggs
2 tablespoons chopped parsley
salt and freshly ground black pepper

1. Heat the oil in a large frying pan, add the onion and cook until softened.

2. Meanwhile, drain the artichokes and cut them into quarters. Finely grate the Parmesan, then very lightly whisk three-quarters of it with the eggs, parsley and seasoning. Stir in the artichokes.

3. Pour the egg mixture into the pan and cook over a low heat for about 10 minutes until the frittata is set most of the way through but the top is still creamy.

4. While the frittata is cooking, preheat the grill to very hot.

5. Sprinkle the remaining cheese over the frittata and put it under the grill for a couple of minutes.

SPINACH AND EGGS

SERVES 2

The eggs are simply cooked on a bed of spinach, with cheese sprinkled over the top. Instead of feta cheese, you could use goat's cheese, Gruyère, mozzarella or fontina cheese.

Sliced mushrooms fried with the onion are a good addition. If you are using the oven for another dish, the eggs can be baked in individual ovenproof dishes at 180°C/350°F/Gas Mark 4 for about 15 minutes.

2 tablespoons virgin olive oil
1 clove garlic, finely chopped
3 spring onions, white parts and a little of
   the green parts, finely chopped
450g (1lb) fresh spinach

4 eggs
75–115g (3–4oz) feta cheese
black pepper
paprika to serve

1. Heat the oil in a heavy frying pan, add the garlic and spring onions and fry for 2–3 minutes. Stir in the spinach until it has wilted.

2. With the back of a spoon, make 4 depressions in the spinach mixture. Add an egg to each depression. Finely crumble the cheese over the eggs and spinach and grind pepper over.

3. Cover the pan and leave to cook for 5–10 minutes until the eggs are set to your liking. Sprinkle with paprika and serve.

TORTILLA

SERVES 4–6

Cooking a tortilla can be speeded up if you start with cooked potatoes. A traditional tortilla should contain just eggs and potatoes and perhaps onions, but I often add other flavourings, even if only some garlic or chopped herbs – parsley is the most typically Spanish. Chopped peppers, courgettes, broad beans, artichokes preserved in oil and grated cheese are also my favourite additions. When I'm not in a hurry after cooking the potatoes and onions, I drain off and reserve the oil, then mix them with the egg, in a bowl, and leave for 10–15 minutes. Enough oil is then poured into the pan to make a thin film, and the egg mixture added to cook as below. The tortilla can be served with Red and Yellow Pepper Relish (see page 63), Light Tomato Sauce (see opposite), Aïoli (see page 30) or, especially if parsley is not included in the tortilla, Green Sauce (see opposite). Wedges of cold tortilla are ideal for picnics or for including in packed meals. If you would like to serve one of the sauces mentioned above, pack it in a separate container.

6 tablespoons olive oil	5 eggs
400g (14oz) potatoes, diced	salt and freshly ground black pepper
1 Spanish onion	
leaves from a small bunch of parsley (optional)	

1. Heat the oil in a large, heavy, preferably non-stick frying pan, add the potatoes and seasoning, cover and cook over a low heat for 15–20 minutes.

2. Meanwhile, chop the onion and stir into the potato as it is cooking, covering the pan again. Stir occasionally to prevent sticking.

3. Chop the parsley leaves, if using, then lightly beat with the eggs.

4. Pour the egg mixture evenly over the potato mixture, immediately stirring it in. Cook over a moderate heat, shaking the pan from time to time, until the underside is set and beginning to brown.

5. Cover the pan with a large, warm plate and hold it in place with one hand. Quickly invert the pan so the omelette slips out on to the plate.

6. Slide the omelette back into the pan, uncooked side down. Continue to cook until the underside is lightly browned.

Green Sauce

Mix together 1 finely chopped shallot, 1 finely chopped small clove garlic, 4 tablespoons chopped parsley, 2 tablespoons chopped mixed herbs such as thyme, chervil, rocket, tarragon, basil and marjoram, ½–1 tablespoon chopped salt-cured capers, grated zest of ½ lemon (optional), 75ml (3fl oz) virgin olive oil, and white wine vinegar and seasoning to taste.

The sauce can be made in advance without the vinegar and kept covered in the refrigerator; the herbs darken when the vinegar is added. Double the quantity can easily be made so that you have some ready as a stand-by.

Light Tomato sauce

Heat 2 tablespoons olive oil in a frying pan and fry 1 chopped shallot until softened. Add 4 chopped, ripe, well-flavoured tomatoes and 2 tablespoons medium bodied dry white wine. Cook over a high heat for 2–3 minutes. Season and add 2 tablespoons chopped chives.

Individual Spinach 'Tortas'

Serves 2

'Tortas' translates as cakes and these are the fried kind, a cross between a French omelette and an Italian frittata. They can be eaten with Tomato and Red Pepper Sauce (see page 37), Red and Yellow Pepper Relish (see page 63), or Greek yogurt, or slipped into a buttered country-style roll or bap.

250g (9oz) young spinach leaves
2 eggs
2 teaspoons freshly grated Parmesan
   cheese

about 2 teaspoons chopped parsley,
   marjoram or thyme
olive oil for frying
salt and freshly ground black pepper

---

1. Wash but do not dry the spinach leaves, then chop them. Put into a pan and heat, stirring, until wilted and there is no water visible. Tip into a colander and squeeze hard to expel surplus water.

2. Lightly beat the eggs with the Parmesan, herbs and seasoning, then stir in the spinach.

3. Heat a thin film of oil in a frying pan, add spoonful of the spinach mixture and spread out to about 9cm (3½ inches) in diameter. Cook until lightly browned on both sides.

4. Remove and repeat with the remaining mixture.

*H*ERB 'FRITTERS'

SERVES 2

I was served these tender, herby fritters in the south of France for a light lunch dish, accompanied by a tomato salad and good bread. Back home I have served them as a first course partnered by Red and Yellow Pepper Relish (see below) or Tomato and Red Pepper Sauce (see page 37). They can also be served as a main course with Ratatouille (see page 35) or Peperonata (see page 34).

The herbs can include parsley, a little sorrel, basil, tarragon, thyme, chives, fennel, mint and chervil.

a bunch of herbs (see above)	50g (2oz) pine nuts, finely chopped
1 clove garlic	(optional)
115g (4oz) soft cheese	olive oil and/or butter for frying
75ml (3fl oz) crème fraîche	salt and freshly ground black pepper
3 eggs	

1. If using sorrel, chop it finely. Chop the remaining herbs with the garlic.

2. Put the cheese into a bowl then stir in the crème fraîche, followed by the eggs. Stir in the herbs, and pine nuts, if liked, and season to taste.

3. Heat a thin film of oil and/or butter in a frying pan and spoon in the mixture to make approximately 10cm (4 inch) wide and 1.25cm (½ inch) thick 'fritters'. Cook gently for about 4 minutes a side.

4. Serve warm.

Red and Yellow Pepper Relish

Chop 1 small red pepper and 1 small yellow pepper into small pieces less than 6mm (¼ inch) square. Mix with ¼ red onion, finely diced, 1–2 tablespoons balsamic vinegar, and a little chopped garlic and herbs, if liked. Season and cover with virgin olive oil. Leave for 2 hours. If liked, strain off excess oil to serve (the oil can be used for salad dressings).

The relish can be kept in a covered container in the refrigerator for a few days.

CHAPTER 2

Salads & Vegetable Dishes

Salad ingredients are at their flavourful, colourful best in summer so I make as much use of them as I can, serving them for main courses as well as for first courses and side dishes. Things have moved on since the days when a salad meant uncooked limp lettuce leaves, a slice or two of cucumber, flavourless tomato and rubbery hardboiled egg. Now salads can be made of cooked ingredients – vegetables such as peppers, aubergines, courgettes, tomatoes and even onions, that have been grilled (preferably over a charcoal fire) are especially popular in summer. They can be served warm or left to cool so that the flavours meld together. Salads can also be made from pulses combined with garlic, herbs and good olive oil plus other suitable ingredients and they too may be served hot or cold. Accompanied by good bread, all these dishes are ideal vegetarian main courses.

The kaleidescope of the summer vegetable harvest with its rich flavours provides many other tasty main course dishes. Laced with fragrant herbs or aromatic spices, these are satisfying to eat because of the intensity of their flavours, yet not too heavy.

ORANGE AND DATE SALAD Ⓥ

SERVES 4

Sweet, juicy oranges can be used to make many refreshing salads for serving at the beginning of a meal as well as at the end.

---

3 large, juicy oranges, peeled and thinly
    sliced horizontally
8 fresh dates, stones removed, quartered
8 blanched almonds, slivered, toasted if
    liked

½–1 tablespoon orange flower water
ground cinnamon for sprinkling (optional)

---

1. Lay the orange slices on a shallow serving plate. Scatter the dates and almonds over them.

2. Sprinkle with the orange flower water, and cinnamon, if liked. Cover and chill lightly.

White Bean Salad

Serves 2

Cannellini and borlotti are types of haricot beans found in Italy. Cannellini, which are slightly fatter than our normal haricots, feature in Tuscan cooking and are particularly good with the region's richly flavoured olive oils. The colour of pretty borlotti beans can vary from pale cream to bright pink-brown, but they are always mottled with red and brown. To give the salad a Middle Eastern flavour, use coriander instead of parsley, and serve with pitta bread.

425g (15oz) cannellini or borlotti beans, drained and rinsed
juice of ½ small lemon
4 tablespoons extra virgin olive oil
1 red onion

1 well-flavoured tomato
2 tablespoons finely chopped parsley
salt and freshly ground black pepper
about 6–9 oil-cured black olives and 1 boiled egg, quartered, to garnish

1. Put the beans into a saucepan, add water to almost cover, cover the pan and heat over a moderate heat, shaking the pan occasionally, until the beans are warmed through.

2. Drain the beans well, then immediately mix with the lemon juice, olive oil and seasoning. Leave to cool, or at least while you finely chop the onion, and peel and chop the tomato.

3. Stir the onion, tomato and parsley into the beans. Serve garnished with the olives and egg quarters.

COS AND CROUTON SALAD
WITH CHEESE DRESSING

SERVES 4

Sometimes, instead of adding the garlic to the dressing, I add a whole clove, halved lengthways, to the butter and oil mixture when I fry the croûtons (I then discard the garlic, but you could eat it, if you like). Bread with herbs is good for this salad.

3 slices of firm bread	**dressing**
1 tablespoon olive oil	½ clove garlic
25g (1oz) unsalted butter	65g (2½oz) Roquefort cheese
2 heads of Cos lettuce	2 tablespoons crème fraîche
freshly ground black pepper	6 tablespoons virgin olive oil
chopped parsley or chives to serve	3–4 teaspoons sherry vinegar

1. To make the dressing, drop the garlic into a blender while the motor is running, then add the remaining ingredients and mix together until fairly smooth.

2. Cut the crusts from the bread and cut the bread into cubes. Heat the oil and butter in a deep frying pan, add the bread and stir to coat well. Fry until golden, stirring occasionally. Transfer to paper towels to drain.

3. Tear the lettuce into pieces and put into a salad bowl. Pour the dressing over it and scatter with the croûtons. Grind pepper over the top and sprinkle with parsley or chives.

CHICORY WITH BLUE CHEESE DRESSING

SERVES 4

I was served this salad in Spain while researching some of that country's excellent local cheeses, which are more or less unknown elsewhere because the production is so small. This recipe uses one of the better, though not well known cheeses, the blue Cabrales, a fairly pungent cheese that is usually made from cow's milk though ewe's or goat's milk may be added. Look for Cabrales in specialist cheese shops or good delicatessens. If it is not available, use a good Roquefort (not a small prepackaged wedge).

Depending on the mayonnaise and your taste, you may like to sharpen the dressing with a little lemon juice, and a drop or two of milk may be needed to thin it.

3 heads of chicory

Dressing
40g (1½oz) Cabrales
about 2 tablespoons crème fraîche or
   Greek yogurt

4–6 tablespoons mayonnaise
2 tablespoons chopped parsley
salt and cayenne pepper

1. To make the dressing, mash the Cabrales, then mix in the crème fraîche or yogurt followed by the mayonnaise. When thoroughly mixed, stir in the parsley and salt and cayenne pepper to taste.

2. Slice the chicory into rings and put on to a deep serving plate.

3. Spoon the dressing over the chicory.

Goat's Cheese and Rocket Salad

Serves 4

Warm, just melting, goat's cheese and a pungent rocket dressing make a positive start to a meal, or a satisfying snack if served with country bread.

115g (4oz) rocket

25g (1oz) almonds

1 clove garlic

3 tablespoons freshly grated Parmesan cheese

7 tablespoons virgin olive oil

1 tablespoon walnut oil

1 teaspoon sherry vinegar

115g (4oz) corn salad

40g (1½oz) walnut halves

4 slices of goat's cheese log with rind

salt and freshly ground black pepper

1. Preheat the grill. Put half of the rocket, the almonds, garlic, and Parmesan in a blender or food processor. Turn on the motor and slowly pour in 6 tablespoons of the olive oil. Season and set aside.

2. Whisk together the remaining olive oil, the walnut oil, vinegar and seasoning and toss with the remaining rocket and the corn salad. Divide between 4 plates.

3. Grill the walnuts until brown and crisp, then scatter around the edges of the salads.

4. Put the goat's cheese on a foil-lined baking sheet and cook as close to the grill as possible for 1–2 minutes until browned. Using a fish slice, transfer one slice to the centre of each plate. Spoon the rocket sauce on top and serve immediately.

Wilted Spinach, Cheese and Olive Salad

Serves 2–4

Croûtons (see page 68) can be added to make a more substantial salad.

450g (1lb) small spinach leaves
2 shallots, finely chopped
1 clove garlic, finely chopped
1 tablespoon chopped mint
10 black olives, preferably oil-cured,
   stones removed, halved

175g (6oz) feta cheese
4 tablespoons virgin olive oil
1½ tablespoons red wine vinegar
black pepper

1. Toss the spinach with the shallots, garlic, mint and olives. Crumble the cheese over the top and grind black pepper over.

2. Heat the oil in a frying pan until it is almost smoking. Quickly pour over the salad and toss together so that as many leaves as possible are coated. Immediately pour the vinegar into the hot pan, then trickle it over the salad. Toss again and serve.

SLICED AUBERGINE SALAD ⓥ

SERVES 2

These aubergine slices bathed in a garlicky dressing can be eaten while warm or, if there is time, they can be left to cool (but not in a refrigerator) so that the ingredients and flavours have time to marry together. Serve with plenty of good bread to mop up dressing.

1 large aubergine
75ml (3fl oz) virgin olive oil, plus extra for brushing
4–5 cloves garlic

1 tablespoon lemon juice
1 teaspoon wholegrain mustard
about 8 basil leaves
salt and freshly ground black pepper

1. Preheat the grill. Cut the aubergine into slices about 6mm (¼ inch) thick slices. Brush with oil and grill for about 3 minutes a side until they are tender, brown and crisp on the outside.

2. Meanwhile, blanch the garlic in boiling water in a small saucepan for 2 minutes, then drain. Return to the pan, cover with cold water and simmer until tender.

3. Arrange the aubergine slices, overlapping them slightly as necessary, in a large shallow dish.

4. Drain the garlic and put into a blender with the lemon juice and mustard. With the motor running, slowly pour in the 75ml (3fl oz) oil as when making mayonnaise. Season and adjust the levels of flavourings, if necessary.

5. Pour over the aubergine slices and scatter with the basil leaves. Grind more black pepper over the slices, if liked.

GRILLED ONION SALAD

SERVES 2

Grilling takes the bite out of the onions and develops their natural sweet taste. You will need some wooden cocktail sticks to hold the onion slices together (don't use plastic ones as they will melt); the sticks also make turning the slices easier.

2 large Spanish onions, cut into 2cm (¾ inch) slices
virgin olive oil, mixed with an equal amount of pesto if liked, for brushing
rocket leaves

40g (1½oz) pecorino, romano or Parmesan cheese
1½ tablespoons extra virgin olive oil
1½ teaspoons lemon juice
salt and freshly ground black pepper

1. Preheat the grill. Push a wooden cocktail stick through each onion slice from one side to the other, to hold the rings together. Brush both sides with oil and lay them in a single layer on the grill rack. Season the top sides and grill, turning occasionally, until a rich dark brown and just beginning to char (the ends of the cocktail sticks may also char).

2. Using a fork to steady the onion slices, pull out the cocktail sticks. Separate the onions into rings.

3. Make a bed of rocket leaves in a shallow dish and scatter the onions over them. Shave the cheese over them.

4. Whisk together the extra virgin olive oil, lemon juice and seasoning and pour over the salad.

POTATO, LIME AND CORIANDER SALAD ⓥ

SERVES 4

This simple, lively tasting salad makes an appetising change from more traditional potato salads. It can be served warm, but if time allows, or you are able to plan ahead, the potatoes can be left to cool in, and soak up, the dressing.

450g (1lb) small new potatoes, or small waxy potatoes such as Pink Fir Apple, Charlotte, Ulster Sceptre or Pentland Javelin, halved or quartered according to size
1 clove garlic, halved

a sprig of coriander
4 spring onions
1 lime
3 tablespoons virgin olive oil
2 tablespoons coarsely chopped coriander
salt and freshly ground black pepper

---

1. Cook the potatoes with the garlic and coriander sprig in boiling, salted water until the potatoes are tender; the time will depend on the size of the potatoes.

2. Meanwhile, chop the spring onions. Coarsely grate the zest of about three-quarters of the lime.

3. Squeeze the lime to get 1½ tablespoons of juice. Whisk the juice with the oil, seasoning and lime zest.

4. Drain the potatoes well, discard the garlic and the coriander sprig and immediately toss the potatoes with the dressing and, if serving immediately, the spring onions and chopped coriander.

5. If preparing the salad in advance, leave the potatoes to cool in the dressing. Toss with the spring onions and coriander just before serving.

GARLIC BREAD SALAD

SERVES 3-4

This full-flavoured salad is a good way of redeeming French bread that is past its best, or was not very good in the first place. You can, of course, use bread that has nothing wrong with it.

½ French stick
1 small clove garlic
about 25g (1oz) unsalted butter
salad leaves such as spinach, rocket, curly endive or Cos lettuce
6–8 black olives, preferably oil cured

Dressing
leaves from a small handful of parsley sprigs
25g (1oz) sun-dried tomatoes in oil, drained

5 tablespoons oil from the sun-dried tomatoes **or** virgin olive oil **or** a mixture of virgin olive oil and oil from the tomatoes
2 tablespoons red wine vinegar
1–2 drops Tabasco sauce to taste
1 teaspoon sun-dried tomato paste
2 tablespoons freshly grated Parmesan cheese
salt and freshly ground black pepper

1. Preheat the grill. Mix all the ingredients for the dressing, except the Parmesan, in a blender. Add the Parmesan and mix very briefly.

2. Cut the bread into thick slices and toast on one side.

3. Meanwhile, crush the garlic and beat into the butter.

4. Spread the butter over the untoasted side of the bread, then grill until golden.

5. Meanwhile, tear the salad leaves into pieces and put in a salad bowl. Halve the olives.

6. Cut the bread into cubes and add to the bowl with the olives. Pour over the dressing and toss together.

RED PEPPER AND CROUTON SALAD

SERVES 4

The amount of water for the dressing depends on the thickness of the mayonnaise you are using. If the oven is on, you could bake the bread at about 200°C/400°F/Gas Mark 6 for 8–10 minutes until crisp and golden.

1 small–medium Cos lettuce
3 red peppers
virgin olive oil for frying
4 slices of country bread about 2.5cm
  (1 inch) thick
1 plump clove garlic

4 tablespoons mayonnaise
2½ tablespoons freshly grated Parmesan
  cheese
freshly ground black pepper
thinly shaved Parmesan cheese and basil
  leaves to serve

1. Preheat the grill. Tear the lettuce into large pieces and put in a shallow salad bowl. Cut the peppers in half lengthways, then grill until charred and blistered.

2. Meanwhile, heat a thin layer of oil in a large frying pan. Cut the bread into 2.5cm (1 inch) cubes and fry until crisp and golden. Drain on paper towels.

3. While the bread is cooking, drop the garlic into a blender or food processor while the motor is running, then add the mayonnaise, grated Parmesan and 2–3 tablespoons water. Season with pepper and set aside.

4. Remove the charred skin from the grilled peppers, then cut them into strips and toss with the lettuce.

5. Add the hot croûtons to the salad, trickle the dressing over, scatter with the shavings of Parmesan and the basil leaves and serve.

WARM LENTIL AND CORIANDER SALAD ⓥ

SERVES 2

For an even quicker salad, drain a 400g (14oz) can of lentils, then heat through gently in enough water to just cover them. Drain before mixing with the dressing.

225g (8oz) green or brown lentils	4 spring onions
a small bunch of coriander	2 tablespoons white wine vinegar
1 bay leaf	6 tablespoons extra virgin olive oil
1 clove garlic	salt and freshly ground black pepper

1. Bring a saucepan of water to the boil. Add the lentils, 2 of the coriander sprigs and the bay leaf. Return to the boil, then simmer for 15–20 minutes until the lentils are tender.

2. Meanwhile, finely chop the garlic and spring onions. Chop the remaining coriander leaves.

3. Whisk together the vinegar, oil, garlic, spring onions and seasoning.

4. Drain the lentils and discard the bay leaf and coriander sprigs. Mix the lentils and chopped coriander with the dressing while the lentils are still warm. Serve.

Variation
Use mint instead of coriander.

77

WARM LENTIL, BULGAR AND SESAME SALAD Ⓥ

SERVES 4

Individually, grains, pulses and seeds are valuable sources of nutrients for vegetarians, but when combined they complement each other to make the outcome better than the sum of the parts. However, this salad has far more going for it than just being good for you – it is also delicious.

175g (6oz) brown lentils
175g (6oz) thawed frozen peas
150g (5oz) bulgar
2–3 tablespoons sesame seeds
a bunch of mint
a bunch of parsley

a bunch of spring onions
1 clove garlic
2 lemons
115ml (4fl oz) virgin olive oil
salt and freshly ground black pepper

1. Bring a saucepan of water and a kettle of water to the boil.

2. Add the lentils to the saucepan and simmer for 15–20 minutes until tender, adding the peas for the last 4–5 minutes. (Quickly return the water to the boil after adding the peas, then reduce it to a simmer again.)

3. Put the bulgar into a bowl and stir in the boiling water from the kettle. Leave to soak.

4. Meanwhile, toast the sesame seeds in a heavy, dry frying pan until fragrant. Set aside. Finely chop the herbs and spring onions. Crush the garlic. Grate the zest from the lemons and squeeze out the juice.

5. Drain the lentils. Drain the bulgar, quickly squeeze out excess water and mix all the ingredients together. Serve.

Couscous Salad Ⓥ

This colourful, well-flavoured salad is simple to prepare and takes only minutes. It is satisfying as it is, but it is very adaptable and if you want to make it more substantial, add some diced feta cheese. Other ingredients such as chopped cucumber, red peppers, courgettes, aubergines or capers – anything you fancy – can also be added. The salad can be prepared ahead and kept, covered, in the refrigerator, return it to room temperature about 45 minutes before serving.

175g (6oz) couscous	2 tablespoons chopped coriander
2 large, well-flavoured tomatoes	2 tablespoons chopped parsley
5 spring onions	1 tablespoon chopped mint
2 cloves garlic	2 tablespoons virgin olive oil
4 halves of sun-dried tomato	2 tablespoons lemon juice
75g (3oz) oil-cured black olives	salt and freshly ground black pepper

1. Soak the couscous in 175ml (6fl oz) water for about 10 minutes until all the water has been absorbed. Crumble the grains with your fingers to separate them.

2. Meanwhile, chop the tomatoes, spring onions and garlic. Thinly slice the sun-dried tomatoes. Remove the stones from the olives.

3. Mix all the ingredients together.

*I*TALIAN RICE SALAD

SERVES 4

This salad makes a satisfying, richly flavoured first course. The amounts of pesto, lemon juice and seasoning may vary according to the brand of pesto you use.

450ml (16fl oz) vegetable stock or water	2–3 tablespoons extra virgin olive oil
125g (4½oz) arborrio rice	3 tablespoons lemon juice
150–175ml (5–6fl oz) pesto	salt and freshly ground black pepper
2 cloves garlic, halved lengthways	shaved Parmesan cheese and shredded
5 spring onions, chopped	basil to serve

1. Bring the stock or water to the boil in a shallow saucepan or deep frying pan with a lid. Stir in the rice, about one-quarter of the pesto, the garlic and spring onions and bring to the boil. Cover the pan, lower the heat and cook gently without removing the lid for 20 minutes until the rice is tender and the liquid absorbed.

2. Pour the rice into a serving bowl and discard the garlic. Stir in the oil, remaining pesto and lemon juice, and seasoning to taste.

3. Scatter the shavings of Parmesan and the shredded basil over the salad.

*F*ATTOUSH Ⓥ

SERVES 4 *as a main course, 6 as a first course or side salad*

Like Tabbouleh (see page 82), fattoush is a herby Lebanese salad that varies from cook to cook. And again, the variations are almost always in the quantities of ingredients, with one exception: this time, purslane. Authentically, fattoush should contain this herb but it may not always be available. You may find purslane in the summer in Middle Eastern or Greek Cypriot shops.

---

2 large, well-flavoured tomatoes, chopped
6 spring onions, whites and some green parts chopped
1 clove garlic, chopped
about 10cm (4 inches) of cucumber, diced
1 small Cos lettuce, torn into 1.25cm (½ inch) lengths

4 tablespoons coarsely chopped parsley
2 tablespoons chopped mint
2 tablespoons chopped coriander
6–7 tablespoons virgin olive oil
2–3 tablespoons lemon juice
1–2 pitta breads
salt and freshly ground black pepper

---

1. Preheat the grill. Toss together the tomatoes, spring onions, garlic, cucumber, lettuce, herbs, oil, lemon juice and seasoning.

2. Split the pitta breads and toast with the opened sides upwards until brown and starting to become very crisp. When cool enough to handle, tear the breads into small pieces and toss lightly with the salad. Serve immediately.

*T*ABBOULEH Ⓥ

SERVES 4 *as a main course*

Although there are almost as many different recipes for this Lebanese salad as there are people who make it, it is the relative quantities of ingredients that change, rather than the choice of ingredients. Tomatoes are the exception. Some people (and I am one of them) include them but others do not. If time allows, mix the soaked and squeezed couscous with the lemon juice, parsley, spring onions and seasoning and leave in the refrigerator for 1 hour before adding the remaining ingredients.

225g (8oz) couscous	2 large, well-flavoured ridged tomatoes
50g (2oz) parsley	4 tablespoons lemon juice
8 spring onions	4 tablespoons extra virgin olive oil
about 10cm (4 inches) cucumber	salt and freshly ground black pepper
leaves from 40g (1½oz) mint	crisp lettuce leaves to serve

1. Soak the couscous in cold water to cover for 20 minutes until the grains are soft to the bite. Tip into a large sieve to drain and squeeze out as much water as possible.

2. Meanwhile, finely chop the parsley, spring onions, cucumber and mint. Chop the tomatoes.

3. Pour the couscous into a bowl and stir in the lemon juice, parsley, spring onions and seasoning.

4. Stir the remaining ingredients, except the lettuce leaves, into the salad. Line a shallow bowl with the lettuce leaves, then spoon in the salad.

Feta and Bulgar Salad

Serves 3–4

The wonderful mix of textures and taste in this salad mean that it turns up frequently on my kitchen, dining-room and garden tables throughout the summer months. It appears as a first course, snack or light main course, or as part of a buffet spread. It also goes into packed meals.

175g (6oz) bulgar
1 clove garlic
a small bunch of spring onions
1/3 cucumber
1 red pepper
115g (4oz) feta cheese
3 tablespoons chopped parsley

1½ tablespoons chopped mint
3 tablespoons virgin olive oil
2 tablespoons lemon juice
salt and freshly ground black pepper
oil-cured black olives and lemon wedges
 to garnish

1. Soak the bulgar in water to cover for 15 minutes.

2. Meanwhile, chop the garlic, spring onions, cucumber and red pepper. Finely crumble the cheese.

3. Tip the bulgar into a sieve and squeeze it dry.

4. Mix all the ingredients together, except the garnish. Serve garnished with the black olives and lemon wedges.

Stuffed Fennel

SERVES 6 *as a first course, 4 as a main course*

Braised fennel with cheese, almonds and tomatoes is a classic dish, but here, instead of cooking the fennel in a tomato sauce, sun-dried tomatoes are included in the stuffing. I have found this to be more popular and always well received, whether it is served hot or cold. Nectarine Galettes (see page 128) are suitable for serving after the fennel, as they make use of the oven.

6 small fennel bulbs
squeeze of lemon juice or a few drops of
    vinegar
tablespoon olive oil
25g (1oz) unsalted butter
1 onion, finely chopped

6 halves of sun-dried tomato packed in
    oil, drained
150g (5oz) log of goat's cheese
25g (1oz) almonds
salt and freshly ground black pepper

1. Preheat the oven to 200°C/400°F/Gas Mark 6. Bring a large saucepan of salted water to the boil while you prepare the fennel. Cut off and reserve the feathery fronds. Cut the bulbs in half vertically.

2. Add lemon juice or vinegar to the water, then add the fennel. Cover and simmer for 8–10 minutes until tender.

3. Meanwhile, heat the oil and unsalted butter in a small frying pan, add the onion and fry until soft.

4. While the onion is cooking, chop the sun-dried tomatoes quite finely and mix into the cheese with the almonds and seasoning.

5. Drain the fennel, reserving the cooking liquid. Put the fennel, cut-side uppermost, in large, shallow baking dish.

6. Stir the onion into the cheese mixture and pile on to the fennel halves. Pour the reserved cooking liquid into the dish to a depth of about 5cm (2 inches). Put into the oven for 15 minutes. Garnish with the reserved fennel fronds and serve.

MIXED GRILLED VEGETABLES Ⓥ

SERVES 2

I particularly like this combination of grilled aubergines, peppers, tomatoes and garlic, which tastes even better if cooked over a barbecue so they have that oh so appetising, unmistakable smoky taste. The dressing is Spanish, but could just as easily be Italian if balsamic vinegar is used, or could have a North African or Middle Eastern flavour if a pinch of roasted and ground cumin seeds is added to the oil, and white wine vinegar used instead of sherry vinegar.

1 small aubergine
4 tablespoons virgin olive oil, plus a little for brushing
1 red pepper
2 well-flavoured tomatoes

3 plump cloves garlic, unpeeled
2 teaspoons sherry vinegar
salt and freshly ground black pepper
chopped parsley and country bread to serve

1. Preheat the grill. Slice the aubergine into rounds. Lay the slices on the grill rack and brush with oil. Add the red pepper, tomatoes and garlic and brush them with oil. Grill, turning as necessary, until the aubergine slices are browned and tender and the skins of the pepper and tomatoes are charred and blistered. The garlic skin should be charred and the inside soft. Remove the vegetables as they are ready.

2. Transfer the aubergine slices to a deep serving plate. Leave the other vegetables until they are cool enough to handle.

3. Peel the pepper, cut it into strips and add to the plate; reserve any juices. Peel the tomatoes, and deseed if liked. Slice the flesh and add to the plate. Add the tomato juices to the pepper juices.

4. Peel the garlic and mix to a paste with a pestle and mortar. Beat in the vinegar, followed by the 4 tablespoons oil. Add the reserved juices and seasoning. Pour over the salad. Sprinkle with parsley and serve warm or cold with country bread.

CAPONATA Ⓥ

SERVES 4–6

This sweet and sour Sicilian dish is often served cold as an antipasto, but I like to serve it hot with good bread as a lunch or supper dish. Any leftovers will be good eaten cold the next day.

4 tablespoons olive oil	2 teaspoons capers, preferably salt-packed
2 small aubergines, diced	3 tablespoons chopped parsley
5 sticks of celery	4 tablespoons red wine vinegar
1 onion	1–2 tablespoons sugar
6 well-flavoured tomatoes	salt and freshly ground black pepper
12 green or black olives	

1. Heat 3 tablespoons of the oil in a heavy frying pan, add the aubergines and fry until soft and browned. Using a slotted spoon, remove to a bowl.

2. Meanwhile, slice the celery and finely chop the onion.

3. Add the remaining oil, the onion and celery to the pan and fry until the vegetables are brown and soft.

4. While the vegetables are cooking, chop the tomatoes. Stir them into the browned vegetables and simmer for about 15 minutes until the sauce is thick.

5. Stone and quarter the olives and stir into the thick sauce with the aubergines, capers, parsley, vinegar and seasoning. Add sugar to taste to make a good balance of sweet and sour.

STUFFED BABY AUBERGINES Ⓥ

SERVES 4 *allowing 3 halves per person*

Packed with vegetables and nuts, these stuffed baby aubergines are fresh tasting, flavourful, and satisfying without being heavy. The length of the method is deceptive because each individual step is listed separately, but when cooking you will find they all interlock nicely.

6 baby aubergines	2 well-flavoured tomatoes
virgin olive oil for brushing	1 tablespoon chopped coriander
1½ tablespoons olive oil	1 tablespoon chopped parsley
4 spring onions, chopped	15g (½oz) walnuts, chopped
1 clove garlic	2 tablespoons finely chopped walnuts
115g (4oz) brown cap mushrooms	salt and freshly ground black pepper

1. Preheat the grill. Cut the aubergines in half lengthways, leaving the stalks intact. Deeply score the aubergine flesh with a sharp knife, but do not pierce the skin. Season the cut-side with pepper and brush with virgin olive oil. Grill, cut-side up, until soft and lightly browned. Leave the grill on when the aubergines are done.

2. Meanwhile, heat the 1½ tablespoons olive oil in a frying pan, add the spring onions and fry until softened.

3. Chop the garlic and add to the spring onions as they cook.

4. Chop the mushrooms and add to the spring onions when they are soft.

5. Holding the aubergines in a tea towel, scoop out the flesh with a teaspoon, leaving the shells intact. Put the shells in a shallow, heatproof serving dish. Chop the aubergine flesh and stir into the mushrooms. Leave to cook while chopping and deseeding the tomatoes. Stir the tomatoes into the pan, with the herbs, 15g (½oz) chopped walnuts and seasoning.

6. Remove the pan from the heat and divide the vegetable mixture between the aubergine shells. Scatter the 2 tablespoons finely chopped walnuts over the aubergines and put under the grill for about 5 minutes.

STUFFED COURGETTES

SERVES 2

These stuffed courgettes are lighter and more delicate than many. When they are made with cooked rice, as many are, they can have a tendency to be rather heavy and not very inspiring.

3 medium–large courgettes
175g (6oz) feta cheese
1 egg plus 1 egg yolk
1½ tablespoons chopped parsley

leaves from 2 small sprigs of thyme,
    chopped
freshly ground black pepper

1. Bring a saucepan of water to the boil. Cut the courgettes in half lengthways and scrape out the seeds using a teaspoon. Put the courgette halves, cut-side uppermost, in a steaming basket or colander over the saucepan of boiling water, cover and steam for about 5 minutes until they have softened slightly.

2. Meanwhile, preheat the grill to medium. Crumble the cheese, then mix in the egg, egg yolk, herbs and pepper.

3. Transfer the courgettes to the grill rack. Divide the cheese mixture between the courgettes and cook under the grill until the tops are well browned.

LEEKS WITH TOMATOES AND OLIVES Ⓥ

SERVES 3-4

As it stands, served with good bread to mop up the juices, this dish is ideal for a light summer lunch dish, but it can be made into a more substantial main course by sprinkling fresh breadcrumbs and a mixture of freshly grated Parmesan cheese and mozzarella cheese over the top, and putting it under a preheated grill until browned.

2 tablespoons olive oil

450g (1lb) slim leeks, cut into 4–5cm (1–1½ inch) lengths

1–2 cloves garlic

4 well-flavoured tomatoes

14 black olives, preferably oil-cured

1 small lemon

salt and freshly ground black pepper

chopped parsley to garnish

good bread to serve

1. Heat the oil in a frying pan large enough to take the leeks in a single layer. Add the leeks and cook over a fairly low heat, turning the leeks occasionally, for about 5 minutes.

2. Meanwhile, chop the garlic and tomatoes. Halve the olives and remove the stones.

3. Add the garlic, tomatoes and olives to the leeks, cover and simmer for 10–15 minutes until the leeks are tender. If there is surplus watery liquid toward the end of the cooking, uncover the pan and increase the heat.

4. While the mixture is simmering, grate the zest from the lemon, squeeze out the juice and add both to the pan.

5. Season. Garnish with the chopped parsley and serve with good bread.

SPICED PARSNIPS ⓥ

SERVES 4

Carrots are more usually used for this sweet-spicy dish, but I like to cook parsnips this way. That is not to say that it is not also good with carrots. It is; so try it with both vegetables.

675g (1½lb) young parsnips	¾ teaspoon harissa (see page 5)
1 small onion	100ml (3½fl oz) vegetable stock
3 tablespoons olive oil	¾ teaspoon clear honey
1 clove garlic	a squeeze of lemon juice (optional)
¾ teaspoon coriander seeds	salt and freshly ground black pepper
¾ teaspoon cumin seeds	chopped coriander to garnish

1. Bring a saucepan of water to the boil. Slice the parsnips and add to the boiling water. Cover, return quickly to the boil, then simmer for 7 minutes. Drain well.

2. Meanwhile, finely chop the onion. Heat the oil in a frying pan, add the onion and cook gently until softened.

3. Finely chop the garlic and add to the onion while it is cooking. Stir in the coriander and cumin until fragrant, then stir in the harissa followed by the parsnips.

4. Add the vegetable stock and honey and cook for 7–10 minutes until the parsnips are tender and the liquid is reduced to a sauce.

5. Season to taste and add a squeeze of lemon juice, if liked. Serve garnished with the chopped coriander.

ARTICHOKES AND BROAD BEANS IN OLIVE OIL ⓥ

SERVES 4

My visit to Crete coincided, I'm happy to say, with the artichoke season and, glutton that I can be, I tried them in many different ways without tiring of them. (I don't know whether it was the local variety or the growing conditions, or a combination of both, that made them taste so good.) I ate this version on a terrace beneath the vines outside a taverna near Fourfouras. A loaf of chewy local bread was served to mop up the copious, richly flavoured juices. A snooze in the sun followed.

About 4 tablespoons virgin olive oil, preferably Greek (or substitute some of the oil from the artichokes for some of the oil), plus a little for serving (optional)

4 spring onions, white parts and a little green of the green parts, chopped

2 cloves garlic, crushed

6–8 artichokes in oil, drained

450g (1lb) thawed frozen broad beans or shelled fresh broad beans

3 tablespoons chopped dill, mint or parsley

½ lemon

salt and freshly ground black pepper

firm white bread to serve

1. Heat the oil in a saucepan, add the spring onions and garlic and cook until softened, but not coloured.

2. Meanwhile, cut the artichokes into quarters.

3. If using fresh broad beans, add them to the pan with the dill, mint or parsley and 2 tablespoons water. Bring to the boil, cover tightly and simmer for 5 minutes.

4. Add the artichokes to the pan. If using thawed frozen beans, add them as well, together with the dill, mint or parsley and 2 tablespoons water. Bring to the boil, cover and simmer, shaking the pan occasionally, for 4–5 minutes or until the beans are tender and the artichokes are heated through. Add seasoning and a good squeeze of lemon juice to taste; add some oil, if liked, and serve with firm white bread.

BROAD BEANS AND POTATOES
BRAISED IN TOMATOES Ⓥ

SERVES 4–6

A simple, but tasty and sustaining dish. If you have any leftover, you'll find it is very good served at room temperature the next day. Packed into a container with a tight-fitting lid, it can be taken as part of a packed meal or picnic.

2 tablespoons virgin olive oil
1 onion, finely chopped
2–3 cloves garlic, chopped
300g (10oz) new potatoes, or small waxy
  potatoes, halved or quartered
  according to size
675g (1½lb) well-flavoured, ripe
  tomatoes
1 tablespoon sun-dried tomato paste

350g (12oz) shelled broad beans, or
  frozen broad beans, thawed
1½ tablespoons chopped dill
1 tablespoon chopped parsley
salt and freshly ground black pepper
1–2 tablespoons extra virgin olive oil to
  serve (optional)
chopped parsley to garnish

1. Heat the oil in a large saucepan, add the onion and garlic, and cook until softened but not coloured. Stir in the potatoes, cover and cook, shaking the pan occasionally, for 5 minutes.

2. Meanwhile, seed and chop the tomatoes then stir into the potatoes with the sun-dried tomato paste. Bring to the boil then simmer, un-covered, until the potatoes are about half cooked.

3. Add the broad beans, dill and parsley and cook for a further 10 minutes, stirring occasionally, until the beans and potatoes are tender and the tomatoes reduced to a thick sauce. If the sauce seems rather watery towards the end of cooking, increase the heat and boil hard until it becomes the right thickness. Season.

4. Serve with extra virgin oil stirred in, if liked, and garnish with the chopped parsley.

OKRA IN TOMATO SAUCE ⓥ

SERVES 4

Middle Eastern dishes containing okra are often simply called '*bamia*', the ethnic name for okra, no matter what other ingredients they contain. Very often the okra are cooked in a tomato sauce, to which lamb will sometimes be added. Small pods are preferred. When trimming okra, it is important not to pierce the inner seed pods as this releases the gelatinous substance they contain.

3 tablespoons olive oil
1 onion
450g (1lb) small okra pods
2 cloves garlic
4 large, well-flavoured tomatoes
1 bay leaf

2 tablespoons chopped parsley
2 teaspoons sun-dried tomato paste
  (optional)
a squeeze of lemon juice (optional)
salt and cayenne pepper
chopped parsley to garnish

1. Heat the oil in a frying pan, add the onion and fry until just beginning to brown.

2. Meanwhile, trim the okra and chop the garlic.

3. Add the okra and garlic to the pan and fry until flecked with brown.

4. While the okra and garlic are cooking, chop the tomatoes.

5. Stir the bay leaf into the pan and cook until it is fragrant, then add the tomatoes, parsley, and salt and cayenne pepper. Simmer for about 15 minutes, stirring occasionally, until the tomatoes are soft enough to break up.

6. If the tomato flavour is not strong enough, add sun-dried tomato paste. Add a squeeze of lemon juice, if liked, and serve garnished with the chopped parsley.

FENNEL AND TOMATO GRATIN

SERVES 4

Aniseed-flavoured young fennel simmered in a light tomato sauce, finished with a savoury, crisp cheese-and-breadcrumb topping and with a final scattering of toasted almonds, is an invitingly 'moreish' dish. It can also be served at room temperature.

2–3 tablespoons virgin olive oil	2 halves of sun-dried tomato (optional)
2–3 small fennel bulbs, total weight about 450g (1lb), sliced, a few feathery fronds reserved	40g (1½oz) Parmesan cheese
	50g (2oz) mozzarella cheese
	1½ tablespoons fresh breadcrumbs
1 onion	2 tablespoons flaked almonds
2 cloves garlic	salt and freshly ground black pepper
4 large, well-flavoured, ripe tomatoes	

1. Heat the oil in a frying pan, add the fennel and cook, stirring, for about 4 minutes.

2. Meanwhile, chop the onion and garlic and add to the fennel while it is cooking.

3. Chop the tomatoes and sun-dried tomato, if liked, then stir into the pan and cook, uncovered, over a low heat, stirring as necessary, until the fennel is very soft. Season.

4. While the vegetables are cooking, preheat the grill. Grate the cheeses and mix with the breadcrumbs and black pepper.

5. Transfer the fennel mixture to a shallow, heatproof dish and sprinkle the cheese mixture over the top. Put under the grill until bubbling and beginning to turn golden. Scatter with the flaked almonds and return to the grill until the almonds are browned. Garnish with the reserved fennel fronds.

SPANISH POOR MAN'S POTATOES Ⓥ

SERVES 4

I have come across a number of recipes with this name. Some are slight variations of this old Castillian one, while others differ quite substantially and may include, for example, tomatoes, bacon or eggs. This version goes well with poached eggs or simple omelettes or it can be served on its own with crisp salad.

2–3 tablespoons olive oil

1 teaspoon paprika

675g (1½lb) potatoes, sliced

1 Spanish onion, finely chopped

1–2 cloves garlic, chopped

salt and freshly ground black pepper

chopped parsley to serve

1. Heat the oil in a heavy flameproof casserole, stir in the paprika until mixed in, then stir in the potatoes, onion, garlic and seasoning. Cook, stirring occasionally, for about 5 minutes, then add about 115ml (4fl oz) water.

2. Bring to the boil, cover tightly and simmer gently for 10–15 minutes, stirring occasionally, until the potatoes are tender.

3. Serve sprinkled generously with parsley.

SESAME VEGETABLE CASSEROLE

SERVES 4

For this dish a selection of root vegetables is simmered in a tahini-enriched stock, then Greek yogurt is stirred in to make the self-made sauce creamy. Sesame seeds enhance the nutty taste.

4 tablespoons olive oil

3 cloves garlic, chopped

2 onions, sliced

225g (8oz) kohlrabi, chopped

2 carrots, chopped

225g (8oz) potato, chopped

225g (8oz) small turnips, chopped

450ml (15fl oz) vegetable stock

4 tablespoons tahini

115g (4oz) frozen peas

3 tablespoons sesame seeds

3 tablespoons chopped coriander

150ml (5fl oz) Greek yogurt

salt and freshly ground black pepper

1. Heat the oil in a large, heavy-based saucepan, add the garlic and all the vegetables, except the peas, and fry, stirring frequently, over a high heat until the vegetables are beginning to brown and soften.

2. Stir a little of the stock into the tahini, then stir this mixture and the remaining stock into the vegetables. Bring to the boil, then cover and simmer for about 20 minutes until the vegetables are tender; add the peas towards the end of the cooking.

3. Meanwhile, if liked, preheat the grill and spread out the sesame seeds on a baking tray. Toast the seeds, stirring occasionally, until lightly browned.

4. Add the coriander and sesame seeds to the pan, then gradually stir in the yogurt. Season and heat through gently without allowing to boil.

CHAPTER 3

Grains & Pulses

Grain and pulse dishes provide many vegetarian main courses, and I have found that many that I serve in summer come from around the Mediterranean. Which, on reflection, is not too surprising. The weather there is what summer weather should be and these ingredients are staples of Mediterranean cooking because meat is not a main item in the diet. The cooks in each country have therefore exploited grains and pulses to their full potential, so leading to an enormous range of tasty dishes. Italian cooks learnt a long time ago how best to cook the local round-grain rice to make creamy textured risottos which are a far cry from the fragrant pilaffs of the Middle East. In North Africa wheat is turned into couscous, in the Middle East, Greece and Turkey it is used for bulgar, while in Italy it is turned into pasta. Add each nation's favourite flavourings, herbs or spices and the result is a group of widely differing dishes.

COUSCOUS WITH DRIED APRICOTS
AND ALMONDS ⓥ

SERVES 4

You can stir butter or olive oil into the couscous in the traditional way, or serve it without.

175g (6oz) couscous
40g (1½oz) blanched almonds
50g (2oz) no-need-to-soak dried apricots
salt and freshly ground black pepper

chopped coriander to garnish
unsalted butter or olive oil to serve
 (optional)

---

1. Preheat the grill. Soak the couscous in 175ml (6fl oz) water for about 10 minutes until all the water has been absorbed.

2. Meanwhile, lightly toast the almonds, stirring so that they brown evenly, then coarsely chop them. Slice the apricots. Bring a saucepan of water to the boil.

3. Rub the couscous through your fingers to remove any lumps, then mix in the apricots and seasoning. Tip into a steaming basket or metal colander lined with muslin, cheesecloth or fine cloth, cover tightly, then put over the saucepan of boiling water and heat for 15–20 minutes.

4. Fluff up the couscous with a fork, mixing in the almonds, coriander and butter or olive oil, if liked, at the same time.

WARM BULGAR WITH MIXED VEGETABLES Ⓥ

SERVES 2

This makes an attractive main course that is filling, but not heavy. If you have time, instead of frying the red pepper you can grill it until it is charred and blackened, then peel it and cut it into strips. The vegetables can be varied: for example, you can use grilled aubergines, baby corn or sliced onions.

115g (4oz) bulgar
1 clove garlic, halved
3 tablespoons olive oil
2 small courgettes
1 small, fleshy red pepper
115g (4oz) mixed oyster and shiitake
  mushrooms
50g (2oz) sun-dried tomatoes in oil,
  drained

½ fresh red chilli
115g (4oz) artichokes in oil, or canned
  artichokes, drained and halved
75g (3oz) black olives, preferably
  oil-cured
salt and freshly ground black pepper
chopped parsley to garnish

1. Soak the bulgar in plenty of boiling water to cover in a covered bowl while preparing the vegetables.

2. Preheat the grill. Heat the garlic in 2 tablespoons of the oil in a large frying pan until it is fragrant. Remove from the heat.

3. Meanwhile, slice the courgettes lengthways, put into a bowl, pour the remaining oil over them and stir to coat. Grill until browned and tender.

4. While the courgettes are grilling, slice the red pepper, mushrooms, sun-dried tomatoes and chilli (discard the chilli seeds, if liked).

5. Return the frying pan to the heat and scoop out and discard the garlic. Add the pepper, mushrooms, sun-dried tomatoes and chilli to the pan and sauté for about 3 minutes. Stir in the artichokes, olives and courgettes, add the seasoning and cover and warm through for a minute or so. Remove from the heat.

6. Drain the bulgar, quickly squeeze out the excess water and spoon into a shallow serving dish. Pile the vegetables on top and garnish with the chopped parsley.

SPICED BULGAR WITH ALMONDS Ⓥ

SERVES 2

Ideally, whole spices that have been toasted in a dry frying pan until fragrant and then freshly ground, should be used rather than commercially ground ones from a jar. If you use spices frequently, they can be toasted and ground, perhaps once a week or so.

115g (4oz) bulgar
a small bunch of spring onions
1 clove garlic
2 tablespoons olive oil
¾ teaspoon ground cumin
¾ teaspoon ground coriander

¼ teaspoon ground allspice
2 large, well-flavoured tomatoes
a bunch of mixed parsley and mint
40g (1½oz) roasted almonds
grated rind and juice of ½ lemon
salt and freshly ground black pepper

1. Soak the bulgar in plenty of hot water to cover.

2. Meanwhile, chop the white and green parts of the spring onions. Chop the garlic.

3. Heat the oil in a frying pan, add the spring onions and garlic and spices. Fry until the vegetables have softened.

4. While the vegetables are cooking, chop the tomatoes. Discard the coarse stalks from the herbs and chop the remainder.

5. Drain the bulgar and squeeze out excess water. Stir the spiced vegetables, tomatoes, almonds, lemon rind and juice, herbs and seasoning into the bulgar.

BULGAR PILAFF WITH AUBERGINES AND CHEESE

SERVES 3-4

Bulgar pilaffs can be made more quickly and easily than their rice counterparts, and make an interesting change. This is one of my favourites. Instead of haloumi cheese, you could use feta or goat's cheese or, unauthentically, Italian taleggio or fontina cheese.

2 tablespoons olive oil
1 aubergine, cut into 1cm (½ inch) cubes
225g (8oz) bulgar

75–115g (3–4oz) haloumi cheese, cut into small cubes
salt and freshly ground black pepper
coriander leaves to garnish

1. Heat the oil in a deep frying pan, add the aubergine and fry until tender. Using a slotted spoon, transfer to paper towels to drain. Keep warm.

2. Pour the oil from the pan. Add the bulgar and 225ml (8fl oz) water, cover and simmer for 5 minutes.

3. Stir the aubergine into the pan, season, then cover and heat through. Scatter the cheese over the top of the pilaff, grind black pepper over, cover the pan and leave off the heat for a few minutes so the cheese begins to melt.

4. Garnish with the coriander leaves and serve immediately.

FRAGRANT PILAFF ⓥ

SERVES 4

The spices turn not-very-exciting plain boiled rice into an exotic-flavoured dish that tastes extravagant, but costs very little extra and takes up very little of your time.

2 tablespoons olive oil	2 bay leaves, torn
2.5cm (1 inch) cinnamon stick	1 small onion, finely chopped
seeds from 4 cardamom pods	225g (8 oz) long-grain white rice
3 cloves	salt and freshly ground black pepper
1½ teaspoons cumin seeds	

1. Heat the oil in a large, heavy, flameproof casserole, add the spices and bay leaves, and stir until fragrant. Stir in the onion and cook fairly gently, stirring occasionally, until softened.

2. Bring 570ml (1 pint) water to the boil.

3. Stir the rice into the onion mixture until well coated, then slowly pour in the water. Take care as it will splatter. Add the seasoning and bring to the boil. Cover tightly and cook gently for 10 minutes, without lifting the lid.

4. Remove from the heat and leave for a further 10 minutes, without uncovering. Fork up the rice and serve.

*F*ENNEL *P*ILAFF Ⓥ

SERVES 3-4

Although it is not traditional, I am partial to some cheese stirred into the pilaff just before it is served; freshly grated Parmesan, finely chopped feta or goat's cheese, or grated taleggio or fontina are all good.

40g (1½oz) butter
1 onion, chopped
1 fennel bulb, finely chopped, feathery
   fronds reserved
1 clove garlic
570ml (1 pint) vegetable stock or water

1 red pepper
225g (8oz) long-grain rice
a pinch of saffron threads
3 tablespoons sesame seeds
salt and freshly ground black pepper

1. Heat the butter in a saucepan, add the onion and fennel, and fry for about 3 minutes.

2. Meanwhile, chop the garlic, then add to the pan while the vegetables are frying.

3. Bring the stock or water to the boil. Chop the red pepper.

4. Stir in the rice and red pepper so that the rice is well-coated with butter, then add the stock or water and return to the boil.

5. While waiting for the pan to come to the boil, crush the saffron threads. Add to the pan.

6. Stir the boiling rice once, cover the pan and cook gently, without lifting the lid, for 15 minutes.

7. Meanwhile, toast the sesame seeds.

8. Remove the rice from the heat, remove the lid and cover the rice with a clean tea towel. Leave for 5 minutes.

9. Fork the sesame seeds, reserved fennel fronds and seasoning through the rice.

GREEN, RED, BLACK AND WHITE PILAFF Ⓥ

SERVES 4

This is a very cheery dish that makes the best of colourful, seasonal vegetables and proves that it is not necessary to spend ages adding extra garnishes to make food look appetising.

570ml (1 pint) vegetable stock
225g (8oz) long-grain rice
675g (1½lb) mixed green vegetables such as peas, broad beans, French beans, asparagus tips, sugar snap peas and mangetout
1 clove garlic
1 red pepper
5 pieces of sun-dried tomatoes in oil, drained

12 black olives, preferably oil-cured, stoned
1½ tablespoons oil from the sun-dried tomatoes
2–4 tablespoons chopped mixed herbs
salt and freshly ground black pepper
chopped coriander and/or parsley to serve

1. Bring the stock to the boil in a saucepan. Bring a large saucepan of water to the boil.

2. Stir the rice into the stock, return quickly to the boil, stir, cover and simmer for 15–20 minutes until the rice is tender and the stock has been absorbed.

3. If using French beans or sugar snap peas, cut them into about 5cm (2 inch) lengths. Add the vegetables to the pan of boiling water, cover, return quickly to the boil and simmer until tender. Drain well.

4. Meanwhile, crush the garlic. Chop the pepper and slice the sun-dried tomatoes. Halve the olives.

5. Heat the oil in a large frying pan, add the garlic, pepper and sun-dried tomatoes and cook for 3–4 minutes. Stir in the rice until well-coated, then add the green vegetables, olives, herbs and seasoning. Heat, stirring, for about 1 minute. Serve liberally scattered with the parsley and/or chopped coriander.

RED SPANISH RICE WITH PEPPERS

SERVES 4

The peppers are halved and laid on top of spiced rice that has been made red with sun-dried tomato paste, or tomato purée. To cut down on the preparation, you can use bottled peppers.

570ml (1 pint) vegetable stock or water	a pinch of chilli powder
1 clove garlic	4 tablespoons virgin olive oil, plus extra to
3–4 red and yellow peppers	serve (optional)
225g (8oz) long-grain rice	3 tablespoons sun-dried tomato paste or
2 teaspoons paprika	tomato purée
1 teaspoon ground cumin	chopped parsley to serve
1 teaspoon ground coriander	

1. Preheat the grill. Bring the stock or water to the boil in a wide, shallow heavy-based pan. Chop the garlic. Halve the peppers lengthways.

2. Grill the peppers until the skins are charred and blistered.

3. Stir the rice, garlic, paprika, cumin, coriander, chilli powder and 4 tablespoons oil into the pan. Return quickly to the boil, then cover and simmer for about 10 minutes.

4. Leave the peppers until cool enough to handle, then peel off the skins.

5. Stir the sun-dried tomato paste or tomato purée into the rice and quickly lay the peppers, cut-side down, over the surface of the rice. Cover the pan and continue to simmer gently until the rice is tender and the liquid has been absorbed.

6. Remove from the heat and leave, covered, for 5 minutes.

7. Scatter with the chopped parsley, and trickle oil over the rice, if liked, to serve.

Risottos

The aim when making a risotto is to cause the rice – which must be Italian arborio or, better still, carnaroli – to absorb hot stock gradually so that it swells into evenly cooked grains that are bound creamily together, neither too runny nor too dry.

Throughout the cooking, keep the stock just simmering. The best utensil for adding the stock to the rice is a soup ladle. Adjust the heat beneath the pan of rice so that it is bubbling happily. If it is too high, the liquid will evaporate too quickly and the rice will not cook evenly; if it is too low, the risotto will become gluey. With the correct heat, the rice should be ready to eat in about 25 minutes. You may have to adjust the amount of liquid you add each time to achieve the correct creamy consistency, and you may find that you need a little more or less liquid in total.

RISI E BISI

SERVES 4

This is a favourite Italian dish that can be described as a very thick soup or a runny risotto; but it is not a risotto with peas. It sounds a humble dish, but it used to be served at the Doge's Palace as part of a banquet held to celebrate St Mark's day, 25 April, when the first of the season's fresh green peas were available from the vegetable gardens around the lagoon. In my kitchen, frozen *petits pois* usually have to do duty as stand-ins for fresh ones.

50g (2oz) unsalted butter
1 onion, finely chopped
850ml (1½ pints) vegetable stock
200g (7oz) arborio rice
300g (10oz) frozen petits pois

3 tablespoons chopped parsley
40g (1½oz) freshly grated Parmesan cheese
salt and freshly ground black pepper

1. Heat the butter in a saucepan, add the onion and fry until softened and pale gold.

2. Meanwhile, bring the stock to the boil.

3. Stir the rice into the pan with the onion until well coated with oil, then stir in the stock. Cover and simmer for about 15 minutes until the rice is just tender to the bite. Stir occasionally and add the peas and parsley towards the end of cooking.

4. Season the rice, pour into a serving dish and stir in the Parmesan.

Mushroom Risotto

SERVES 4

Do use one of the mushrooms listed in the ingredients, or wild mushrooms, rather than ordinary white ones which really do not have enough flavour. About 150ml (5fl oz) medium-bodied dry white wine can be used instead of the same amount of stock; use it as the first liquid addition.

75g (3oz) unsalted butter
1 tablespoon olive oil
450g (1lb) mushrooms, such as brown
  cap, shiitake or oyster mushrooms, or a
  mixture, broken or cut into large pieces
1 clove garlic, chopped

350g (12oz) arborio rice
about 1.1 litres (2 pints) hot stock or
  water
50g (2oz) freshly grated Parmesan cheese
salt and freshly ground black pepper

1. Heat half of the butter and all the oil in a heavy-based saucepan, add the mushrooms and garlic, and cook until the liquid from the mushrooms has evaporated.

2. Stir in the rice until it is well-impregnated with butter, then add a ladleful of hot stock or water. Bring to the boil and stir until the stock has been absorbed.

3. Continue adding ladles of stock or water and simmering until it is absorbed, stirring almost all the time, until all the stock and water has been used. The rice should be just tender but still have a bit of bite, and the risotto should have a silky, creamy consistency that is neither too wet nor too dry.

4. Remove from the heat, stir in the Parmesan, the remaining butter and seasoning, and serve straightaway.

ASPARAGUS RISOTTO

SERVES 4

This is one of the best risottos and a marvellous way of making expensive asparagus go further. To save preparation time, choose slim or fairly slim spears that do not have to be peeled.

50g (2oz) unsalted butter
1 shallot, chopped
350g (12oz) slim asparagus spears
300g (10oz) arborio rice
150ml (5fl oz) medium-bodied dry white wine

about 1 litre (1¾ pints) hot vegetable stock
salt and freshly ground black pepper
freshly grated Parmesan cheese to serve

1. Heat three-quarters of the butter in a large frying pan, add the shallot and fry for a couple of minutes.

2. Meanwhile, cut the tips off the asparagus spears and slice the stems on the diagonal into 2.5cm (1 inch) pieces.

3. Add the stems to the frying pan and cook for 2–3 minutes.

4. Stir in the rice until well-coated with butter. Over a medium heat, add the wine and stir until it has been absorbed.

5. Add a ladleful, or about 150ml (¼ pint), of stock and continue to stir until the stock has been absorbed. Continue adding stock until the rice is tender, but still firm to the bite, and the risotto is creamy. Add the asparagus tips with the second-to-last ladleful of liquid, about 10 minutes before the end of cooking.

6. Remove from the heat and stir in the remaining butter and seasoning. Serve at once with a fairly generous amount of freshly grated Parmesan sprinkled over the risotto.

*I*TALIAN RICE WITH CHEESE AND BASIL

SERVES 4

Unlike risotto, this rice dish can be left to cook unattended. I like to use fontina cheese, which melts beautifully into strands among the rice grains, but you could use mozzarella if you are unable to get fontina. At the end of the simmering, the garlic will be quite mild and can be left in the rice, but I usually tie it in a small piece of muslin (any other piece of clean cloth could be used), so that I can remove it easily after cooking. This makes a good filling, savoury supper or lunch dish, so is more suitable for cooler days than hot ones. I serve a crisp salad afterwards.

300g (10oz) arborio rice	50g (2oz) Parmesan cheese
1–2 cloves garlic, halved	2 tablespoons chopped basil leaves
40–50g (1½–2oz) unsalted butter	salt and freshly ground black pepper
225g (8oz) fontina cheese	

1. Bring a large saucepan of water to the boil. Add the rice, garlic and salt, stir once, then cover and simmer for 15–20 minutes until the rice is tender, but still firm to the bite.

2. Meanwhile, dice the butter. Coarsely grate the fontina and finely grate the Parmesan.

3. Quickly drain the rice and tip it into a warm serving dish. (Hook out the garlic if you like.) Immediately stir in the butter, cheeses, basil and black pepper so that the fontina melts into strands. Serve straightaway.

CHEESE AND BARLEY 'RISOTTO'

SERVES 2

This unconventional version of risotto is easier to make than a standard one, as it does not have to be stirred while it is cooking. With its soft, creamy, almost porridge-like texture and cheesey flavour, it is real comfort food when summer weather lets us down. The risotto must be eaten soon after it is made, otherwise it goes gluey.

A salad-type first course goes well before the 'risotto' and a fruit dessert, such as Melon and Orange Salad (see page 123) or Figs with Raspberry Sauce (see page 121) makes a good ending to the meal.

200g (7oz) pearl barley
75g (3oz) unsalted butter
2 cloves garlic
2 shallots
115ml (4fl oz) medium-bodied dry white
  wine

4 tablespoons whipping or double cream
115–175g (4–6oz) Gorgonzola cheese,
  crumbled
salt and freshly ground black pepper
watercress leaves to serve

1. Measure the volume of the pearl barley, then pour 3 times that amount of water into a kettle. Bring to the boil. Heat half of the butter in a saucepan, add the barley and cook, stirring, until toasted. Pour in the boiling water, stirring, then return to the boil. Cover and simmer for about 20–25 minutes until the barley is tender and all the liquid has been absorbed.

2. Meanwhile, finely chop the garlic and shallots. Quickly add to the barley while it is boiling.

3. Add the wine to the barley when it is almost cooked.

4. Stir the cream into the barley, heat through, then remove the pan from the heat. Stir in the remaining butter, the Gorgonzola and seasoning.

5. Spoon on to warm plates, add the watercress leaves and eat the 'risotto' immediately.

Spaghetti with Olives, Capers, Tomatoes and Basil

Serves 4

The gutsy sauce is a vegetarian version of the traditional *puttanesca*. (This means tart or prostitute; I suspect that quite a few people order the dish without knowing what they are asking for.) Adjust the heat beneath the sauce so that the tomatoes do not burn but neither is the sauce too watery.

2 tablespoons virgin olive oil	1 tablespoon sun-dried tomato paste
2 cloves garlic, chopped	2 tablespoons capers
1 fresh red chilli	a pinch of dried oregano
450g (1lb) well-flavoured tomatoes	325g (11oz) spaghetti
115g (4oz) black olives, preferably oil cured	black pepper
	freshly grated Parmesan cheese to serve

1. Bring a large saucepan of salted water to the boil. Heat the oil in a frying pan, add the garlic and fry for 2–3 minutes.

2. Meanwhile, seed and chop the chilli and add to the garlic as it is frying.

3. Chop the tomatoes, stir into the softened garlic and cook until the sauce is thickened.

4. Remove the stones from the olives and coarsely chop them. Stir into the tomatoes, together with the sun-dried tomato paste, capers and oregano. Leave to bubble and thicken, stirring as necessary.

5. Add the spaghetti to the boiling water, return quickly to the boil, cover and boil according to the instructions on the pack.

6. Drain the pasta in a colander, return immediately to the pan and quickly toss with the sauce. Serve with black pepper ground over the top and accompanied by Parmesan.

TAGLIATELLE WITH TOMATOES, ROCKET AND PARMESAN CHEESE

SERVES 4

Rocket, shavings of Parmesan, cold, fresh tomatoes and hot strands of tagliatelle make a delicious combination of tastes and textures. The first three ingredients do not need any cooking, so the dish is extremely quick and easy to make.

3–4 well-flavoured plum tomatoes
50g (2oz) piece of Parmesan cheese
1 large bunch of rocket

3–4 tablespoons virgin olive oil
400g (14oz) fresh tagliatelle
salt and freshly ground black pepper

1. Bring a large saucepan of water to the boil. Chop the tomatoes. Shave off long strips of Parmesan using a potato peeler. Discard tough stalks from the rocket, then put the leaves into a large, warmed serving bowl. Mix in the tomatoes, cheese and oil.

2. Add the tagliatelle and a pinch of salt to the boiling water, cover and return quickly to the boil. Uncover and boil for 2–3 minutes until tender, but still firm to the bite.

3. Quickly tip the pasta into a colander, drain well and add to the bowl. Toss everything together and season to taste. Serve immediately.

CREAMY MUSHROOM PENNETTE

SERVES 4

This dish is cooked like a risotto (but doesn't take as long). It is a wonderfully moist, creamy pasta dish that is unlike most others.

3 tablespoons olive oil
2 cloves garlic, finely chopped
225g (8oz) brown cap mushrooms, sliced
3 tablespoons chopped parsley
1 litre (1¾ pints) vegetable stock
350g (12oz) dried pennette or tubettini

1 tablespoon dry sherry
115ml (4fl oz) whipping cream
100g (3½oz) Parmesan cheese, freshly
   grated
salt and freshly ground black pepper

1. Heat 2 tablespoons of the oil in a medium frying pan. Add the garlic, mushrooms and 2 tablespoons of the parsley. Fry for about 2 minutes. Remove from the heat and set aside.

2. Bring the stock to simmering point over a low heat.

3. Heat the remaining oil in a large saucepan over a high heat and add the pasta. Cook, stirring, for 3–4 minutes until the pasta turns golden-brown. Add the sherry and heat until evaporated.

4. Lower the heat to moderately high and add enough of the stock to barely cover the pasta. Cook, stirring frequently. Add more stock as necessary to keep the pasta just covered, for about 12 minutes until the pasta is tender but still firm to the bite.

5. Add the cream, heat for 1 minute then remove the pan from the heat and stir in the mushrooms, Parmesan and remaining parsley. Season to taste and serve immediately.

CHICK PEA AND KIDNEY BEAN 'STEW' Ⓥ

SERVES 4

A colourful, well-flavoured mixture of pulses and vegetables of Spanish origin that, when made traditionally, would have been left to bubble gently in a large earthenware cooking pot over a low heat for hours. Lunching on the stew would be followed by a comfortable siesta.

2 tablespoons olive oil	1 × 400g (14oz) can chopped tomatoes
1 Spanish onion, chopped	175g (6oz) mixed frozen peas and
2 cloves garlic	sweetcorn
1 red pepper	1 × 425g (15oz) can chick peas
2 fresh red chillies	1 × 400g (14oz) can red kidney beans
1 teaspoon ground cumin	salt and freshly ground black pepper
½ teaspoon oregano	

1. Heat the oil in a heavy-based saucepan, add the onion and fry until softened and lightly coloured.

2. Meanwhile, chop the garlic, red pepper and chillies (discard the seeds from the chillies, if liked). Add each ingredient to the onion separately as it is cooking.

3. Stir the cumin and oregano into the softened and coloured onion. Add the tomatoes, peas and sweetcorn and bring to the boil. Drain and rinse the chick peas and kidney beans. Add them to the vegetables as you do so.

4. Season, cover the saucepan and simmer the 'stew' for 15–20 minutes, stirring occasionally.

Spanish Chick Peas with Spinach ⓥ

Serves 2

Chick peas are popular in Spain and are sold dried, *en remojo*, and ready-cooked and salted to eat as a tapas. In Madrid, chick peas are honoured with names such as *gabrieles* (angels) and *trompitos* (trumpets).

about 5 tablespoons olive oil

2 aubergines, cut into cubes

1 fresh red chilli

3 cloves garlic

6 well-flavoured tomatoes

1 × 400g (14oz) can chickpeas

1 teaspoon cumin seeds

1 teaspoon crushed coriander seeds

225g (8oz) small spinach leaves

salt and freshly ground black pepper

coriander leaves to garnish

1. Heat the oil in a large saucepan, add the aubergines and fry until golden and soft.

2. Meanwhile, deseed and chop the chilli. Slice the garlic. Chop the tomatoes. Drain and rinse the chick peas.

3. Using a slotted spoon, transfer the aubergine to paper towels to drain.

4. Stir the spices, garlic and chilli into the pan and heat, stirring, for 30 seconds. Add the tomatoes, chick peas, aubergines and enough water to just cover. Bring to the boil then simmer, uncovered, stirring occasionally, for about 15 minutes.

5. Tear the spinach into coarse shreds, stir into the pan and boil for a couple of minutes. Season and serve, garnished with the coriander leaves.

SPICED CHICK PEAS Ⓥ

SERVES 4

Simply heating the tomatoes, rather than simmering them to make a sauce, not only reduces the cooking time but makes the dish lighter and much fresher to the taste.

2 tablespoons olive oil	2 × 425g (15oz) cans chick peas, drained
1 large onion, chopped	and rinsed
2 cloves garlic, chopped	1 tablespoon lemon juice
1 red pepper, chopped	4 tablespoons chopped coriander, plus
1 tablespoon cumin seeds	extra to garnish
500g (1lb 2oz) well-flavoured tomatoes	salt and freshly ground black pepper

1. Heat the oil in a saucepan, add the onion and garlic and cook until golden and soft. Add the red pepper towards the end of the cooking so that it softens a little.

2. Stir in the cumin seeds and cook, stirring, until fragrant. Add the remaining ingredients and heat through, stirring occasionally. Serve garnished with chopped coriander.

Spiced Beans and Mushrooms Ⓥ

Serves 4

I like to use black kidney beans for this recipe (it is only the skins that are black – the fleshy inside is creamy), but the red variety do just as well. Some chopped celery, or red pepper or aubergine, perhaps, can also be added. Serve with good bread.

3 tablespoons olive oil
1½ teaspoons cumin seeds
2cm (¾ inch) cinnamon stick
1 onion, chopped
3 cloves garlic
175g (6oz) chestnut mushrooms
2 x 425g (15oz) cans black or red kidney
  beans

325g (11oz) passata
1½ teaspoons ground coriander
4 tablespoons chopped mixed coriander
  and parsley
salt and cayenne pepper

1. Heat the oil in a flameproof casserole, add the cumin seeds and cinnamon and fry for about 10 seconds. Stir in the onion and cook until beginning to brown.

2. Meanwhile, chop the garlic and add to the pan while the onion is cooking.

3. Halve or quarter the mushrooms depending on size, add to the pan and fry for 2–3 minutes.

4. Drain the beans and add to the pan with the passata, ground coriander, half of the coriander and parsley, and seasoning. Cover and simmer for about 10 minutes, stirring occasionally.

5. Serve sprinkled with the remaining herbs.

CHAPTER 4

Desserts

In warm weather, fruit is often all that is wanted at the end of a meal; plain fruit, or very simple fruit dishes, are my favourite way of rounding off lunch or dinner. When making cold fruit desserts (or, for that matter, any cold dessert), use cold ingredients if possible, and chill the serving dishes. A short time in a freezer helps to lower the temperature quickly. The prepared dessert can also be popped into the freezer until you are ready to eat (unless you are preparing it well in advance, in which case the refrigerator is the appropriate place).

When the weather is less than summery, and if you are feeding pudding fanatics, a proper 'pud' that is not too heavy can go down well. A good rice pudding takes too long to cook, but semolina takes only a few minutes and fits the bill.

GRILLED FRUITS WITH CARDAMOM BUTTER

SERVES 4

Sweet foods as well as savoury ones can be cooked over a barbecue (or under a hot grill). Fruits become extra juicy in the heat, and basting them with butter spiked with cardamom adds an enticing spicy note to their deliciously warm, caramelised flavour.

75g (3oz) unsalted butter, diced
1½ teaspoons lemon juice
seeds from 3 green cardamom pods,
    crushed
1 mango
caster sugar or brown sugar for sprinkling

selection of fruit, such as slices of fresh
    pineapple, bananas halved lengthways,
    halved and stoned apricots or
    nectarines or peaches, thickly sliced,
    peeled pears

1. Preheat the grill. Melt the butter and stir in the lemon juice and cardamom seeds. Set aside.

2. Cut thick slices from each side of the mango stone. Score the flesh in a wide, criss-cross pattern, then push the outside of the skin upwards so that the cuts open out.

3. Put the fruit on the grill rack, brush with some of the butter and sprinkle with the sugar. Cook for 5–7 minutes, turning and brushing with butter occasionally, until the fruit begins to caramelise. Serve straight-away with any remaining butter, including the juices from the grill pan, spooned over the fruit.

*F*IGS WITH *R*ASPBERRY *S*AUCE

SERVES 4

This is one of the simplest desserts, but if it is made with really soft, sun-ripened figs that, skin and all, almost melt in the mouth, it is a truly luxurious sensation. I can easily make a meal of it and eat nearly all this amount myself at one go, but it should serve four people after a meal.

350g (12oz) raspberries
icing sugar or caster sugar to taste
  (optional)

8 really ripe black figs
chilled Greek yogurt to serve

1. Purée the raspberries and pass through a non-metallic sieve. Sweeten to taste, if liked.

2. Slice the figs; or cut them into quarters from top to bottom, leaving them joined at the base, then press your thumb lightly under the base to open them up.

3. Pour the raspberry sauce over the figs and serve with Greek yogurt.

CITRUS SALAD WITH ORANGE
AND HONEY DRESSING ⓥ

SERVES 4

The sharp, fruity tang of lemon juice and grapefruit bring out the sweet taste of large juicy oranges, making this an invitingly fresh, light dessert.

4 tablespoons fresh orange juice

1 tablespoon lemon juice

1–2 tablespoons clear honey

4 large juicy oranges

1 grapefruit

orange flower water

1. Stir together the orange juice, lemon juice and honey until the honey has dissolved.

2. Peel and thinly slice the oranges, or divide into segments. Peel the grapefruit and divide into segments.

3. Put the fruit into a cold bowl, pour the honey dressing over it and sprinkle with orange flower water.

Simple Orange Salad

Peel and thinly slice 6 large juicy oranges, or divide them into segments. Sprinkle the oranges with orange flower water and a light dusting of ground cinnamon.

MELON AND ORANGE SALAD Ⓥ

SERVES 4

The chopped mint does more than make the salad look pretty; it adds a nuance of flavour. Instead of the mint, you could use chopped stem ginger or grated fresh ginger. To make the dessert more special, sprinkle with some dessert wine.

2 ripe Ogen melons	sugar (optional)
3 large juicy oranges	chopped mint to decorate

1. Cut the melons in half and scoop out the seeds. Either scoop the flesh into balls using a melon baller, or roughly scoop it up using a teaspoon. Take care not to pierce the skin.

2. Use a knife to remove the peel from the oranges, then cut down between the flesh and skin of each segment. Ease out the flesh.

3. Toss the orange with the melon and divide between 4 cold dishes. Sprinkle with sugar, if liked, and decorate with the chopped mint.

Vanilla 'Cream' with Summer Berries

SERVES 4

To add an extra touch of luxury, macerate the fruits for a short while in brandy, kirsch or raspberry or strawberry *eau de vie*; it would then be suitable for a dinner party dessert. Sometimes, instead of using vanilla sugar, I use ordinary caster sugar and flavour the cream to taste with rose water.

---

1 egg, separated
3 tablespoons mascarpone cheese
2½ tablespoons vanilla sugar
225g (8oz) ricotta cheese

225g (8oz) mixed berries such as
   raspberries, strawberries, blackberries
   and blueberries
crisp almond biscuits to serve

---

1. Beat the egg yolk, mascarpone and vanilla sugar into the ricotta cheese.

2. Whisk the egg white until stiff but not dry, then lightly fold into the cheese mixture until just evenly combined.

3. Spoon into 4 individual serving dishes and scatter the berries over the top. Serve with almond biscuits.

Chocolate and Chestnut Mousse

Serves 4

A rich and luscious dessert to serve at the end of a lightish meal. Make the mousse before anything else when you start preparing the meal, or prepare it earlier. To speed up the chilling process, pop the filled dishes or glasses into the freezer, or the freezing compartment of your refrigerator.

150g (5oz) good quality, plain chocolate

3 tablespoons brandy

225g (8oz) can sweetened chestnut
  purée

200ml (7fl oz) double cream

4 marrons glacés to decorate (optional)

1. Bring a saucepan filled with a couple of inches or so of water to simmering point, then sit a heatproof bowl on the pan.

2. Meanwhile, chop the chocolate and put most of it into the bowl. (Reserve a small amount for decoration.) As soon as the chocolate melts, remove the bowl from the heat and stir until smooth.

3. Beat the brandy into the chestnut purée. In a separate bowl, whip the cream until soft peaks form.

4. Stir the chocolate into the chestnut mixture, then lightly fold in the cream. Spoon into individual dishes or glasses, and chill lightly.

5. Decorate with the reserved chocolate, and marrons glacés, if liked.

ZABAGLIONE WITH PEACHES OR STRAWBERRIES

SERVES 4

To serve zabaglione, you have to have a short intermission in your meal. It doesn't take kindly to being made in advance (it deflates), and takes at least 10 minutes to cook. (You can have the ingredients ready in advance in a bowl placed over a saucepan.) I find that traditional zabaglione made with egg yolks, not whole eggs, and eaten on its own is far too rich and sweet. When it is made lighter by using mainly whole eggs and served over luscious fruit, it makes a special ending to a meal.

---

4 ripe peaches, halved with the stones
    removed, **or** about 450g (1lb) ripe
    strawberries, hulled
4 tablespoons marsala

25g (1oz) caster sugar
2 whole eggs plus 1 egg yolk
crisp sweet biscuits, preferably almond
    flavoured, to serve

---

1. Divide the fruit between 4 serving bowls or glasses.

2. Bring a saucepan containing about 7.5cm (3 inches) of water to simmering point, and put a heatproof bowl over the pan. Add the marsala and sugar to the bowl, and stir until the sugar has dissolved.

3. Using an electric whisk, whisk the whole eggs and egg yolk into the marsala. Continue whisking until the mixture is very thick; this will take about 10 minutes.

4. Pour over the fruit and serve immediately with crisp, sweet biscuits.

SEMOLINA CREAM

SERVES 4

I serve this old-fashioned pudding as a comfort on days when it has not been anywhere near as hot as I like. The cream can be made as buttery and rich as you like, and instead of flavouring it with rose or orange flower water, you can sprinkle cinnamon over the top just before serving. Some raisins or sultanas can also be stirred in. Alternatively, top generously with chopped bitter chocolate (this is better if the pudding is not too buttery). The pudding can be made before you eat the preceding course because it is usually left to stand for 15 minutes before serving.

about 50–115g (2–4oz) unsalted butter, diced
50g (2oz) semolina
300ml (½ pint) milk

about 50g (2oz) sugar to taste
rose water or orange flower water to taste

1. Melt the butter in a saucepan, preferably non-stick, then stir in the semolina until it is well coated.

2. Stir in the milk and 300ml (½ pint) water and bring to the boil, stirring. Simmer for about 5 minutes, still stirring.

3. Stir in sugar and rose water, or orange flower water to taste. If time allows, leave to stand for 15 minutes before serving.

NECTARINE GALETTES

SERVES 4

This is a quick, hot pudding that is a little more substantial than the others in this chapter. For economical use of the oven, serve the galettes as part of the same meal as 'Stuffed Fennel' (see page 84). Crisp galettes go well with Greek yogurt, fromage frais, crème fraîche, double cream, mascarpone cheese, good vanilla ice cream or the Vanilla 'Cream' on page 124.

225g (8oz) puff pastry

about 1½ tablespoons sieved marmalade
  or apricot jam

4 ripe, but firm nectarines

about 40g (1½oz) unsalted butter

demerara or other brown sugar for
  sprinkling

1 egg yolk, extra melted butter or a little
  milk for glazing (optional)

1. Preheat the oven to 200°C/400°F/Gas Mark 6. Roll out the pastry to 5mm (¼ inch) thick and cut into 4 rounds. Use a saucer or small plate that is about 13cm (5½ inches) in diameter as a guide. Carefully transfer to 2 baking sheets, keeping the shapes true.

2. Spread the rounds with a little marmalade or apricot jam, leaving a 1.25cm (½ inch) border around the edges.

3. Thinly slice the nectarines and arrange them, overlapping, in circles on the rounds, leaving the edges clear.

4. Chop and melt the butter. Brush it over the nectarines and sprinkle with a little sugar. Brush the edges of the pastry rounds with egg, melted butter or milk to make them shiny, if liked. Bake for 20–25 minutes.

Menus

Gazpacho

❖

Spanish Chick Peas with Spinach

❖

Citrus Salad with Orange and Honey Dressing

Red Pepper and Croûton Salad

❖

Stuffed Fennel

❖

Nectarine Galettes

Peperonata

❖

Spaghetti with Olives, Capers, Tomatoes and Basil

❖

Zabaglione with Peaches or Strawberries

Fried Cheese, Olives and Sun-Dried tomatoes

❖

Broad Beans and Potatoes Braised in Tomatoes

❖

Figs with Raspberry Sauce

Cucumber, Mint and Yogurt Soup

❖

Stuffed Baby Aubergines

❖

Grilled Fruits

Grilled Asparagus with Shaved Parmesan

❖

Warm Bulgar with Mixed Vegetables

❖

Melon and Orange Salad

Index

aillade, 27
aïoli, potatoes with, 30
almonds: couscous with dried apricots and almonds, 98
  spiced bulgar with almonds, 100
apricots: couscous with dried apricots and almonds, 98
artichokes: artichoke frittata, 58
  artichokes and broad beans in olive oil, 91
asparagus: asparagus risotto, 108
  grilled asparagus with shaved Parmesan, 29
aubergines: aubergine dip, 20
  aubergine soup, 17
  bulgar pilaff with aubergines and cheese, 101
  caponata, 86
  Moroccan aubergine briouts, 38–9
  ratatouille with mozzarella crostini, 35
  sliced aubergine salad, 72
  spiced aubergines with tomato sauce, 33
  stuffed baby aubergines, 87
  toasted aubergine, tomato and cheese sandwich, 47
  avocado salad, pitta bread with, 48

barley and cheese 'risotto', 110
basil: bruschetta with tomatoes, olives and basil, 44
  egg and basil mayonnaise sandwiches, 41
  Italian rice with cheese and basil, 109
  spaghetti with olives, capers, tomatoes and basil, 111
  sun-dried tomato, cheese and basil crostini, 45
  tomato and basil sauce, 42
beans: bean dip, 23
  bean, tomato and coriander soup, 19
  chick pea and kidney bean 'stew', 114

spiced beans and mushrooms, 117
  white bean salad, 67
blenders, 3
boreks, cheese, 39
bread: bruschetta with tomatoes, olives and basil, 44
  cos and croûton salad with cheese dressing, 68
  egg and basil mayonnaise sandwiches, 41
  garlic bread salad, 75
  goat's cheese on ciabatta, 46
  mozzarella and bread skewers, 42
  mushroom and bread spedieni, 43
  pan bagnat, 49
  pitta bread with advocado salad, 48
  red pepper and croûton salad, 76
  sun-dried tomato, cheese and basil crostini, 45
briks à l'oeuf, 40
briouts, Moroccan aubergine, 38–9
broad beans: artichokes and broad beans in olive oil, 91
  broad beans and potatoes braised in tomatoes, 92
bruschetta with tomatoes, olives and basil, 44
bulgar, 4–5
  bulgar pilaff with aubergines and cheese, 101
  feta and bulgar salad, 83
  spiced bulgar with almonds, 100
  warm bulgar with mixed vegetables, 99
  warm lentil, bulgar and sesame salad, 78
butternut squash soup, 18

cannellini beans: white bean salad, 67
capers, spaghetti with olives, tomatoes, basil and, 111
caponata, 86
cardamom butter, grilled fruits with, 120

132

Other Cookery Titles from Piatkus Books

The Quick After-Work Italian Cookbook
HILAIRE WALDEN

The Quick After-Work French Cookbook
HILAIRE WALDEN

The Quick After-Work Vegetarian Cookbook
JUDY RIDGWAY

The Quick After-Work Pasta Cookbook
JUDY RIDGWAY

Entertaining with Friends: Vegetarian Recipes for all Occasions
SIMON HOPE

Japanese Vegetarian Cookbook
PATRICIA RICHFIELD

Sue Kreitzman's Complete Low-Fat Cookbook

Sue Kreitzman's Low-Fat Vegetarian Cookbook

The Complete Mexican Cookbook
LOURDES NICHOLS

Curry Club Balti Curry Cookbook
PAT CHAPMAN

Curry Club Indian Vegetarian Cookbook
PAT CHAPMAN

For a free brochure with further information on our full range of
titles, please write to: Piatkus Books, FREEPOST 7 (WD 4505), London W1E 4EZ